# Standing on

# Standing on our stories

The Justice, Peace and Wholeness Commitment
of the Iona Community

## Narrator: Susan Dale

wild goose
publications

www.**iona**books.com

Overseas distribution:
Australia: Willow Connection Pty Ltd, Unit 4A, 3-9 Kenneth Road,
Manly Vale, NSW 2093
New Zealand: Pleroma, Higginson Street, Otane 4170, Central Hawkes Bay

Printed by Bell & Bain, Thornliebank, Glasgow

# Contents

# Acknowledgements

This book was born out of a conversation with Peter Macdonald, the then Leader of the Iona Community, who wanted to explain to others 'what the Community was about'. Peter, I have done my best – but there are still so many more stories to tell.

Nothing would have been written at all without the love, prayer, support and contributions of my fellow Community members, who have urged me forward with their inspirational passion and commitment to working for peace and justice in their communities and internationally. They have generously given of their time to talk and write to me. Thank you.

Writing a book with 40 others has not been a simple task but it has been a real privilege. The speed of progress has at times been snail-like, and for this you all have my apologies.

Thanks also to my patient husband, John, who has had to put up with me typing madly and moaning often, and who has also read and corrected many drafts, and to Neil, Sandra and the Wild Goose Publications team for believing that the book was possible.

*Susan Dale*

# Introduction

## From the Rule of the Iona Community

*As members of the Iona Community we commit ourselves to:*

*1. Daily prayer, worship with others and regular engagement with the Bible and other material which nourishes us.*

*2. Working for justice and peace, wholeness and reconciliation in our localities, society and the whole of creation.*

*3. Supporting one another in prayer and by meeting, communicating, and accounting with one another for the use of our gifts, money and time, our use of the earth's resources and our keeping of all aspects of the Rule.*

*4. Sharing in the corporate life and organisation of the Community.*

Two of the questions I am often asked about my work is 'Why do you do what you do?', and 'What exactly does the Iona Community do about justice and peace?'

I have only been a member of the Community for eight years, so in answering these questions I have turned, as always, to my fellow Community members in the hope of understanding more about what the commitment to justice, peace and wholeness means, and how they live this out in their lives.

So, they have started to tell me their stories. Some are written; others are recorded conversations where the narrative is presented in the format of what narrative therapist Christopher Behan describes as a '*speech poem*', for when we speak our stories we do not always talk as we would write but in the rhythm of poetry. The line breaks in the text give the pauses, intonation and rhythm of the spoken word.

In this introduction, I start to tease out what is meant by justice, peace and wholeness. The chapters that follow explore how this is lived out in people's lives.

Annie Sharples' parents are Iona Community members, and Annie grew up and went to school on Iona when her dad was Warden of the Abbey. Annie, her sisters and many other young people who grew up as 'Community kids' have now become a strong young-adult group who continue to support each other personally and in action for justice and peace, despite now being scattered across the UK and beyond. Annie e-mailed me about this:

## Growing up in the Community, Annie Sharples

The Iona Community is not just the beautiful island that gives me a sense of relief and unique joy and calm as soon as I step onto the jetty, but also the supportive, loving and justice-seeking group of wonderful people that makes the Iona Community so important to my life. For me, growing up as part of this community has been cru-cial. It has given me such brilliant opportunities – and friends who mean so much to me; friends who are so like-minded and accepting, who make me feel comfortable and appreciated; that is so impor-tant. We have had conversations that have stuck with me and inspired me. The youth programme has given me many thoughts, challenges and memories: from sharing communion with new friends from across the ocean to staging a protest in support of ref-ugees, marching and singing along the road from the Iona village hall to the MacLeod Centre. The friends I have made through the youth programme have made me realise that, yes, perhaps boycot-ting Nestle and having bulk deliveries of Suma in your garage is not necessarily normal, or cool, but, hey, there are other families who do the same. Being with other young people who are frustrated by, believe in and are grateful for the same things as you, in a society where going to church or deliberately choosing fairtrade or organic products is not the norm, is hugely affirming and important. The shared beliefs and the Rule of the Iona Community are fundamental to many of my personal principles and opinions, such as choosing to use public transport where possible, being active in my support for refugees and opposing nuclear weapons.

Norman Shanks, a former Leader of the Community, gave me some historical context for how the Justice, Peace and Wholeness Commitment became part of our Rule:

## The Justice, Peace and Wholeness Commitment and the Rule, Norman Shanks

While both theologically (the incarnational 'thrust', with the implications of the Gospel for social and political change) and practically, peace and justice concerns have been part of the life of the Community since the outset, it was not until 1966 that this was formulated and formalised as a 'Commitment' and became part of the Rule. It was expanded in 1987-88 into the 'Justice and Peace Commitment' and subsequently amended and updated to cover also, for example, gender justice and sexual orientation. As part of the recent 'membership review' the Rule was revised in 2014 into a four-part form; and alongside this revision a much briefer Justice and Peace Commitment was prepared as a 'holding statement' pending further review; and this is what now appears in the display in the south aisle of Iona Abbey.

Norman went on to tell me about his personal involvement with the Community:

Having been precluded from any form of political or campaigning activity while a 'higher/fast-stream' civil servant (1964-79) in the

Scottish Office, I regarded my membership in the Iona Community (I joined the New members programme in 1979 and was hallowed in 1981) as 'liberation' and immediately joined a working group on justice and peace issues, with its main focus on peacemaking and anti-nuclear campaigning.

My work in the civil service – around policy-making in the fields of local government reform, strategic and local planning, and then criminal justice, and particularly two years working as Private Secretary to successive (Labour!) Secretaries of State for Scotland – conscientised me party-politically but I did not join the Labour Party until later. While studying at New College (1979-82), although I eventually specialised in church history, there were many opportunities both practically and academically to develop my interest in and commitment to justice and peace matters. In ministry – initially as a probationary assistant in an Edinburgh parish and then as Chaplain to Edinburgh University (1983-88), and in my last job before retiring (Govan Old in Glasgow, 2003-07) – I was keen, through worship and Christian education work, to focus on justice and peace themes (for example, One World Week, Christian Aid Week, and so on). Similarly, while lecturing at Glasgow University (Practical theology, 1988-95), justice and peace issues featured significantly within the Christian ethics, church and society, and urban mission courses that I taught.

After I retired from Govan Old, I was, from July 2010-16, a government-appointed, non-executive Director of Greater Glasgow and Clyde Health Board, with a huge remit (more than 40,000 employees, an annual budget of £3bn, big strategic and local challenges, Scotland/Glasgow's abysmal health record and so on). I saw this (and particularly my involvement in discussions about strategic priorities and social problems, best use of limited resources and seeking remedies for health inequalities and combating target/market-driven culture) as part-fulfilment of my commitment to action for justice.

More recently, since October 2015 I have volunteered at the Glasgow North West Citizens' Advice Bureau, offering help to people from a wide range of social, economic and national backgrounds. This has proved an eye-opening, challenging and rewarding experience. It is, I suppose, essentially short-term 'ambulance work' (relating to a variety of needs and problems) but it has increased my awareness of social inequalities and injustice and reinforced my commitment to seeking radical changes in social policies and priorities. And, at congregational level, I was for seven years Convener of the Wellington Justice and Peace Group.

At a personal level I became, and still am, a member of CND, Campaign Against the Arms Trade, Global Justice (formerly World Development Movement), Church Action on Poverty and Medical Aid to Palestinians; from time to time I have taken part in and attended particular events, but on the whole – and currently – my support and involvement has been financial rather than activist.

I am learning that speaking out about injustice is something the Community is good at. Kaz Reeves, a member from the West Midlands, has developed it as part of her ministry.

## Speaking out, Kaz Reeves

My ministry as a priest is unusual.
Wherever I go,
whatever job I take,
it always seems to be to sort out a particular challenge.

I go somewhere, and shortly afterwards I realise that there is clearly what may be considered

an 'elephant in the room'
or there is something that is not right,
and it is often that people have long known the situation
but tolerated it,

because they cannot bear to be the one to sort it,
or because they've come to the job and seen it
and then gone again.

Sometimes it has been going on for years,
but when I arrive, I realise that ...
this just can't go on.

I think it is about justice, and discernment ...
about, when it would be right or the time to act.
I think God sends people into situations at the right time.
I mean ...

When I was a health visitor,
I remember looking at children's files when I was working ...
and I could see that a particular unhelpful situation had been going
on for a long time, and it also seemed really clear to me that

'I am the one who has to deal with it'.
There are also times, however, when I have let things go past,
when I have not acted;
but other times ...

you find yourself on a trajectory for change.

Discernment trains you,
it attunes you to when, and where,
you are called to be active;
whether that is at Faslane, or within your job, or church.

And when you have that realisation that you are called,
and you have people to support you in that,
then you are more able to act.
You are encouraged.

I think the difference is that we are doing this work as part of a community rather than people doing it on their own.

When you can think, 'Oh my goodness, I cannot do this …'
When you are supported in community, you are constantly asking,

'What is the situation here that I am dealing with?'
'What am I called to do?'

Since this happened a few times, I am now less worried about it
than I was.

Not absolutely delighted [laughter], but accepting.

The hallmark is actually … 'Oh shit …'
That moment when you realise
that you keep looking round for somebody else,
and there is no one else.
It has to be you.

And sometimes, it has seemed important to take on the action
because when it comes to something that is not very
straightforward,

the synchronicity of it … means you cannot avoid it.

You can refuse, but you cannot avoid it.
But if you refuse,
you have to live with the consequences of your refusal.
And maybe that is sometimes what you have to do.

That coming together, that synchronicity thing –

I cannot really give a specific example as the situations are often
quite confidential and often where the people or organisations with
the power have colluded …

At the time of crisis, you can often find yourself quite isolated.
You are often isolated from any human power that could help.

You're often on your own with this.
You are looking around for somebody else,
and the powers that be are often almost in opposition.
Not necessarily totally,
but they're passively allowing,
which is actively allowing of course!
Allowing the situation to continue.

And so, then you have to take this active stance.
Do I act?
Do I speak to this person?
Do I write this down?
Something that stops you from being just like somebody else.
It puts you into the spotlight.
Then when you are in the spotlight,
it is very hard, because it then becomes difficult.
You are then often seen as 'stepping out of line' …
and then you wonder if you are doing the right thing.
Are you doing it in the right way?

The thought is always:
do I ignore the elephant in the room, or do I tackle it?
Can I tackle it by myself?
That is why the Iona Community is important.
You can get support from your Iona Family Group,
from the Community.

At a previous church, I remember there were some issues,
but it was good, really, in that case,
that the institution really came alongside me.
There's always a question of when you can engage with
those who hold the power; when that happens, it can be really
transformative and exciting.

You can then see the possibility for change to come.
But there is a lot of work …

In one particular church, for example,
I spent two years just walking around a parish
talking to people,

being told that the church was closed,
which it wasn't ...
being put down,
but feeling that the church was just about hanging on.

Then I realised I could not abandon hope.

I spent some time thinking about it, and when we decided to step forward, the church really took it on.

They became the change-makers themselves.
That time it was about empowering others.

Sometimes, though, it feels like standing in the breach ...

Standing in a spotlight, where you can't see.

I have adapted a bit over the years. Stopped saying, 'Why did that happen?'

And accepting.

Being part of the Community means facing injustice, and one of the hard things spiritually is knowing there is injustice, and you cannot change things.

We are in a sad world where there is injustice.

With age, I think I understand more and more just how sorrow-filled the world is, but how much we're called to move in that.

Having this ministry

is of course easier
because however scared I am
within it

there is the operation
of God at work too somehow.

Strange but it is easier
because the Community
allows that spiritual dimension
to flow, to blossom.

Living in community is about living out our faith,
not just being a community of beautiful people ...

Allowing oneself to be used:
the transformative power of God,
hidden in the support of the Community.

What follows are further personal stories from our Community. They tell how individual members, associate members and others engage with the Rule and its Peace, Justice and Wholeness Commitment, and how we account to each other and support one another in a multitude of ways. The stories are not the 'truth' about Christianity, or the 'truth' about the Iona Community, or even the 'truth' about justice, peace and wholeness. They are merely unique personal reflections that will hopefully enable the reader to catch a glimpse of what it means to be an Iona Community member.

I have acted as a weaver, interlacing the stories together into a narrative account. As the stories are told, further stories emerge. I hope that, as you read this narrative, it resonates with your own life experiences and engagement with peace and justice issues, and that you will learn a little more about the Iona Community. If you share our passion for justice, peace and wholeness, I hope, too, that this book will encourage you, and bring you an awareness that you are not standing alone.

Working for equality, diversity and inclusion

Tony, one of my former counselling clients, once called me a 'bloody social activist'. He was teasing me, referring to the campaigning and writing I did in support of people who are vision-impaired and to enable those who considered themselves on the margins due to mental health difficulties to get the same kind of support services that other people received. It was 2006, and Tony and I were on our way back from a conference, where together we had presented research to a group of top ophthalmologists. The group had been surprised – they had expected me to deliver an academic paper about the mental health problems confronting people affected by severe sight loss. Instead, I brought Tony with me for him to tell *his* story. The ophthalmologists were visibly moved, and wanted to know more. Yet the story Tony told was one these specialists could have heard repeated again and again from any one of their hundreds of patients, if only they had asked. It was a story of courage, of fortitude; but also of loss, of despair, of not being listened to, of not having a voice, of feeling like a second-class citizen who had to be grateful for any small amount of help.

At the time, I was confused and somewhat troubled by the term 'social activist'. Could I be a therapist and a social activist? Could I be a Christian and sometimes take a political stance against injustice? Were these things compatible? Why were the Christian communities I was involved with so silent on so many issues of injustice?

It was at this time that I was starting to engage with the Iona Community as an associate member. The churches I had been to often tried to help the 'poor and disadvantaged' by giving to charity, and by providing things like hearing loop systems and occasionally large-print service books. Was this enough though? What were we doing as church communities to reach out to those with differing needs, views and ways of being, and to work alongside them to create a more inclusive society?

For me, the Iona Community offered an alternative: a way of striving for equality, diversity and inclusion that I had never before witnessed, and within a supportive network of other Christians whose ethical goals were similar to my own.

During my years of membership in the Community, I have learned so much from other members; and also from volunteers, members of staff and guests at the Iona Centres. Guests at the Centres often report that their time on Iona is unique – that it is a place where they encounter inclusion and feel free to be themselves.

I met Alyas when I stayed on Iona for a week as 'Member in Residence', supporting the guests and staff. We started to talk over a cup of tea in the refectory one evening after a service. Later, she e-mailed me a copy of a prayer which she had left in the south aisle of the Abbey Church. Since then we have been in regular correspondence. Alyas wanted me to include her prayer here, as she feels that staying on Iona, and writing this, was a turning point in her life.

## Alyas' prayer

Why, God, have you put me, a Christian,
into the body of an Asian transgender woman?
I call myself Alyas – 'brave one',
but I wish that I did not have to be, or that I was more so.

Why do other Christians exclude, deride and humiliate me?
Which part of the Gospel message says:
I have to be 'cured' rather than loved?
Why do they pray over me, rather than with me?

Where are you, Lord, when I need you?
Alienated now from my family, my birth sex and religion.
Where do I find help?

I found hope for a while on Iona.
For a week, the sea, the white sand,
space to be me.
The love of people around me
allowed a glimpse of what it may mean to be myself
and part of God's family,
accepted for who I am.

Thank you, God, for this place, these people.
Give me the courage to make changes in my life.

*Alyas, while a guest at the MacLeod Centre, 2014*

The following reflection is by Iona Community member Rosemary Power.

## Social justice through disability: Conversations, kindness, duty, malice, stranger danger and State danger, by Rosemary Power

*Conversations*

Sometimes things happen to reverse the expected hierarchies. The casual-seeming conversation with the stranger can be the trigger for exploring the world.

The youngish man on the till that evening wasn't the normal supermarket worker. While he put my purchases through we covered the subjects of Brexit, Trump and immigration. But I needed him to help me to the car, and the conversation went on in the December air.

He'd appeared a born Brit. But he came from the break-up of Yugo-slavia, with a Muslim mother and Serb father. When the war came they were stuck. Before he was nine, two uncles were shot before him, his little cousins killed, their mothers' throats cut. His family fled for Britain – which they had dreamt of as a haven of tolerance and stability. They survived, and arrived, with their memories and nightmares, but alive.

He'd put himself through college, and became an engineer. But when his firm asked him to work in Japan he accepted redundancy rather than leave his wife and young child; and took supermarket work while hoping for another chance to use his skills. Memories of what happened haunted him, and yet made him value his family life the more.

I told him how I, a white Christian, had been writing to a black American Muslim for more than 20 years, first when he was on death row and now in the general prison population; and what I gained from it.

Two strangers in an evening supermarket; the disability that calls for help and allows space for conversation; and the presence of hope. He was a survivor of a war he said 90% of Serbs didn't want, forcing them to drive out their neighbours, which meant also driving out those who were mixed. 'Some day', he said, he might write of it. But only when, and if, he is ready to revisit the dark places of the soul of a nation. We spoke, both carrying our brokenness as the evening darkened around us, and where the soul of this nation was being increasingly pressed into silence.

*Justice can be found in listening to the stories that come from the heart of another, hearing the pain and sharing it. Every refugee has a story, and a contribution to the host nation. Sometimes, disability can offer the context for stories to emerge.*

## Kindness

Sometimes we meet angels, messengers of divine kindness transmitted through humans.

The new battery in the scooter wasn't very good. Over three months, on three occasions, it broke down 500 metres from the home I could see but not reach. I seemed to have no option but a taxi – and an irritated driver on a trip that was too short for metering but without help an impossible one for me.

The first time, Rick loped up. 'Can I help?' asked this big, young man. 'Do you need a push?' I accepted gratefully, wondering how to disentangle myself from him before giving away my address. Then he said: 'I remember you. You bought me a hot dog about a month ago. It was really nice.' I remembered him then too, homeless, hungry, polite but apparently absorbed in his hot dog. The transaction had seemed over. Now he pushed me to the street corner near my door, and took his leave.

A month later, in the same place, my scooter broke down again. A young businessman persuaded a taxi driver to take me to my house; lifted my scooter into the cab; offered to accompany me and take it out; did so, left it on the pavement, assured himself I needed no more help, wished me well and went his way.

The third time was in the evening dark. A young delivery man on a bicycle stopped at once, produced screwdriver and tape, took my battery box to pieces, mended it, wished me well and departed. His repair took me over the bridge; then the problem returned. Again, though filled with the gift of his kindness, I was within sight of a home I could not reach.

Two young men emerged from the pub for a smoke, saw my predicament and offered help. With only a preliminary return inside to safeguard their Friday night beers, they pushed me home. 'Take care,' I said as we passed the police station, 'you're going at more than four miles an hour, the limit for a pavement vehicle, and your alcohol content must be a grey area.' They laughed, and deposited me at the corner by my home, shook hands and left.

Those who helped me came from across the range of the city's ethnic and professional backgrounds. They were bound together in that they each asked, then provided help as it was needed, none of them intruding to my front door. This was a world away from what the State provided just afterwards.

*If justice is setting a part of the world back to its rightness, can it sometimes be found in accepting, in allowing others to offer their kindness in a place of need? The people who helped on each separate occasion did not know that others had also acted in showing the same 'goodness at the heart of humanity planted more deeply than all that is wrong'.*

## Duty

Driving alone through the Lake District, I saw a car on the hard shoulder in front of me. The driver had got out, but was opening the back door. Underneath, invisible to her, the car was on fire. The fuel tank could have exploded at any minute, so I pulled in, got out, shouted, and waved with my crutches, but the wind took my words. When the driver saw me, she stood amazed, unaware of her danger.

I realised that there might be a child in the back seat. My mind told me that I must help get any children out, then we must all get further down the motorway, signalling other cars away. I did not know how much of this I could manage, or how long the adrenalin burst that allowed me to stumble towards her would last. At that moment, a man ran past me with a fire extinguisher. He got down on the ground and put the fire out. A brave, though risky, act.

The driver had only been finding her coat. The white-van driver who had stopped had received the fire extinguisher and training on how to use it only the previous week.

If this incident had happened recently, would I have lost the mobility component of my benefit because of my brief contribution to the drama, for trying to move more than 20 metres? What, if any, is the official position? Should I have ignored the situation? Should I have done nothing and spared myself the pain that followed any exertion? Should I have seen my role as passive, consisting of sympathy and flashing my headlights while people were injured or killed? How would that have engaged with my standing as a citizen, with membership of a Community committed to justice and the Gospel, with my commitment to live as far as I can by the Christian ideal that ultimately asks us to give up our own lives for the sake of another? Trying to run and in doing so breaking a leg in a valid cause seems a small price in comparison. But in a climate of fear and cuts I was glad not to have had to attempt it.

*Justice can be the response of the individual to the needs of other individuals, and no impersonal system should take precedence.*

## Malice

Two days after the first scooter failure, and after 29 years, the mobility allowance that had made my life possible was abruptly withdrawn.

Some three weeks previously I'd had the visit, the one that people in pain dread. We'd heard of what had been happening: the tens of thousands of people on the expensive Motability Scheme who'd had their vehicle taken and sold on; the people thrown upon overstretched mental health services; the people forced out of their jobs because their ability to travel was hacked from under them. Some died without seeing their essential payments restarted. The consequences of the cuts were no secret: the issues had come up time and again in Parliament, though causing scarcely a ripple in the mainstream news.

In my case the assessor asked many questions on private matters, questions I later learned were irrelevant to the assessment; and she did not ask the questions that identify compliance under the current rules. As she stood to leave she offered her hand to be shaken, the ancient symbol of respect and goodwill, and my only physical contact that day. Later she declared, among other debatable matters, that she had tested my handgrip and from this, and other assumptions, she removed the mobility component. My home felt violated, my courtesy denigrated and 30 years of living against pain rubbished by a stranger. Whatever pressures she was under from the private company that employed her, this was wrong. It has since become apparent that this was not an isolated example of attempted trickery.

I'd originally received the allowance after a hard fight, for it was never easy to get. That was at a time when I needed space to grieve my loss of mobility, knowing it would be for life – but this had to wait. It was also a time when attempts to find work, a struggle in itself against pain and weariness, were viewed with contempt. A disabled person was then meant to be invisible, or at best fodder for other people's employment: the presumption that disabled people should themselves work, at their own level, was considered presumptuous. The allowance came at last after the insolence of tribunals and the disdain of some of the senior (but not all of the frontline) staff – and this experience was in no way unique.

When my award was made lifelong, I finally let the tears flow. The journey would still be uphill and with hollows of shadow, but with some financial support, enough to run a car. But, years later, the criteria were changed and everyone had to go through it again, to fit increasingly restrictive demands.

An injustice needs to be made public to warn others; and so does the structure that requires or encourages such actions. A person who has acted unjustly needs to know that there is nevertheless a place for them in the community. A wronged individual is required to forgive on the personal level, and this also occurs within the community. Yet injustice requires challenge. In a wealthy and democratic society, how has the underhand come to dominate, and be so little challenged?

*The tension between personal and public makes Christian living a challenge. It involves finding a balance between the requirement of the Christian to forgive the person who injures, and the responsibility to speak out, in justice for oneself and for others when the structures are at fault. When they restrict our own life and ministry, they also damage those working within the system.*

## Stranger danger

Sometimes disability requires activism of some kind, and sometimes the grace to receive. Some aspects of living with disability can be frightening; others are funny.

Many people with mobility needs have chronic health problems and the onus is on them to prove their needs in a hostile official environment. The physical environment can be daunting too.

Falling over can be a fear, especially for people forced to walk beyond their capacity. A fall in the street may remain unnoticed in a big city, but more often the goodness from strangers will intervene.

We all have stories of people with good intent foregoing the essential preliminary of asking whether help is needed and, if so, what help. There have been those who knocked me down in shops in a rush to the till and then, full of apologies, tried to drag me upright while my body shrank from further contact. There was the healer so full of the power of the Spirit that she almost broke my neck. And one large lady grabbed my left arm and, using her body as a lever, began to haul cheerfully: she nearly dislocated my shoulder.

One year I lost my voice, and one Sunday visited a city church where I was a stranger. To cover the ritual of coffee, I was armed with a notice saying: 'No voice: laryngitis'. When I presented my note I was asked if I was a tourist and, in the absence of a response from me, the person cheerfully continued the conversation in French. They were enjoying themselves so it seemed best to go along with it.

Why are we so seldom asked? Where there is an evident need, the fear of being rebuffed or deemed interfering is a small price to pay for the risk of offering and then asking what to do.

Is there some coarsening of society that has come back, dividing people by fear, just as it divides people into those who have rights and those who deserve less and should be grateful for what is thrown to them? The Syrophoenician woman of the Gospels served Christ by answering from the bottom of the heap, and in doing so stretched our vision of who is to be included in the kingdom of God and afforded respect by society.

*The words 'justice' and 'righteousness' are translations from the same word in Hebrew and in Greek. Righteousness, aligning the self with the will of God, requires listening to God and to our neighbour. Justice requires us to restore the balance between our responsibility to each other and our responsibility to the community.*

### State danger

The State's decisions about how much support, if any, will be given to people with disability, are designed to reduce the budget from which these payments are taken. This leads to various justice issues: on the visibility of disabled people and their right to function as cit-izens, to work and socialise; on how such decisions are made; and on the consequences for society at large.

Without the primary legislation that would at least have brought debate, new criteria are produced every few years, forming a persistent snipping away at allowances so as to exclude. Even calling them 'allowances' raises issues, for this suggests that in some way they are charity rather than an acknowledgement of how certain people have greater financial needs to meet (as with the single person's tax allowance, for example).

Mobility payments come with a raft of other matters, other sources of income, disability parking and so on, which help to provide some freedom and the chance to live in part as other people do, in spite of poverty, acrimony and prejudice. For those who live with pain or whose limbs are absent or do not work, these matter.

The burden of proof falls on those who are ill, limited, or grieving; and on overworked medics. The system, with its internal decisions, gives little space for the human story. No consideration is given to the real costs to those who have their rights and needs 'rejected', or the moral and emotional costs for the people employed to run this system or those who contest it. As well as the depersonalisation of disabled people, those called to apply the rules are deskilled, distressed and in violation of the duties outlined in the wake of the dehumanisation of whole groups of people during the Second World War.

We are not told the criteria by which it was decided who is allowed to be considered disabled. But people do not qualify if they are deemed able to walk more than 20 metres – with or without aids, with or without pain or danger to themselves, which are not regarded as relevant factors. Anyone not deemed to qualify has their funding snatched away without warning.

Many public buildings have no, or insufficient, parking within 20 metres of their doorways. My MP's offices are an example of this, as are the civic offices, cinema and railway station. The chances of a person having public transport this close to their door is unlikely;

the chances of it also coming this close to where they want to go is improbable. Once people are excluded from attending medical appointments and buying food (and using aids or having a heart condition means that they won't be able to carry things without using a car), they are in effect subject to disability discrimination, their civic rights silently withdrawn. As this is the reality of the built environment, it must be that the criteria are at fault.

Whether a private company should be allowed to run an organisation that trades in human pain is another issue to address. The multi-national firms used to assess people do not have a record of competence, either administratively or in terms of assessment; many of their decisions are eventually overturned at costly tribunals. In order to spend less of our money (for we are all taxpayers, through VAT, if nothing else), money from the public purse is drained away, first to private firms and then to the public sector to rectify some of their mistakes.

The financial costs are also shifted silently: onto the health service, through the inevitable falls that lead to treatment in A&E and fracture clinics; onto the social services where costs need to be met from shrinking local budgets; onto the over-pressured voluntary sector; onto mental health services, with their slashed budgets. These are economically expensive ways of shifting budgets around, but the true cost is the destruction of human lives.

Neither the companies nor the State departments seem to have involved disabled people in the design of the new criteria or the training and supervision of those responsible. In a Kafkaesque move, complaints against the companies must be addressed to those same companies, not to the Department for Work and Pensions, which employs them. Yet justice requires that bodies that represent disabled people over whose lives these companies have so much power should be leading the monitoring of them.

During the disability review process, I was offered a compromise in the shape of the lower rate of allowance, which does not come with the same access to other essential support. I declined, partly on the grounds that I could not be less disabled than I had been before, so if the rules had changed it was the rules that were unfit for purpose; and also because, disturbingly, the private company claimed I had 'admitted' something that had never occurred.

*Justice requires the challenging of the unjust structures of society. Disability often isolates people, yet the support of the community can be a crucial factor in bringing injustice to light and seeking to reform it. The telling of the individual story (sometimes supported by statistics) can highlight a wrong because a personal story can communicate the mystery of the individual soul, created in the image of a Creator and Restorer.*

### Afterthoughts

How did one of the 10 biggest economies in the world become determined to exclude people in this manner? How did we manage to make the tax-base too small to pay for the decencies of society? And why have we failed to challenge the making of rules by the anonymous and the unaccountable?

In recent times, hostility to disability has returned. Thirty years after it had seemed to disappear, I experienced it through bullying at a Christian institution because of its insufficient disability parking. We had thought the wheel had turned to create a more civil society.

We are a long way from the actions of Jesus, engaging with and talking to those on the edges, socially and physically; like the woman with the flow of blood; or blind Bartimaeus who other people tried to keep quiet and unnoticed but who took his chance; or the father of the epileptic boy; or the man so possessed with demons that he lived among the tombs, until Jesus gave him peace of mind and the ministry of preaching the good news to others. The Gospel stories about healing are in many ways problematic for people who are sick and disabled, but not at the level of respect and the willingness to have dialogue into which Jesus entered, regardless of a person's economic, social and spiritual status. To Jesus, sick and disabled people were more than the recipients of alms: they were the honoured children of Abraham, created equally by God and designed, like the Lazarus of the parable, for the kingdom of heaven.

How as Christians do we respond to the more general issues of injustice? We have been good at plugging the holes, providing food banks for those who are sanctioned, attacked and made destitute, often for the slightest of reasons, by an increasingly brutal system and people with power and without adequate accountability. One of the reasons why the Ken Loach film *I, Daniel Blake* has proved so effective is because enough people have encountered something of the systemic social failures it addresses. We seem to have created a society that wants to trip people up, to open up gaps under their feet.

Why have we moved against some citizens, with the desire to deny, exclude, reject? Much of the current antagonism is directed towards recent immigrants, but there are also other groups. Disabled people account for about 5% of the population, roughly equivalent in size to the Jews of 1930s Germany, who were similarly prevented from working and engaging in society, and had their civic rights withdrawn, as precursors to so much more. In practice, and without any public challenge, people with no choice in who they are and how they function, fear the knock on the door. This is not the society Jesus calls us to create.

*While this account was in the process of publication, the author had her PIP mobility component restored, after a lapse of several months. Many others have not been so fortunate. Other crucial state payments continue to be cut. On a brighter note, the Scottish Government has gained control over the running of many disability 'benefits', and has entered into a public consultation.*

As Rosemary points out, many crucial state payments continue to be cut and the benefits system for those living with disabilities is often experienced as punitive, rather than enabling all people to have the same advantages in the workplace, at home, during travel or in other situations. We who have disabilities are often seen as demanding, and trying in some way to defraud the British taxpayer. Recently, a man approaching the platform at the rail station, when he saw my white cane, commented: 'I suppose that means if the train is busy you will want me to give up my reserved seat for you, and that my fares cost more so that you can have free travel.'

Fortunately, I had already booked a seat and the train doors opened before I had time to think of a suitable response. Unlike this particular man, who had parked his large car in the station car park, I do not have a choice about how I travel to a work meeting. I am pleased to pay my way, but see my railcard as compensation for the large taxi fare, or having to get a lift from my husband. I need to get me to the station in the first place!

Preaching the Gospel to illuminate issues of equality, diversity and inclusion is something many members do on a regular basis. The following is an extract from a sermon preached by member Mike Holroyd, from Edinburgh, on Transgender Remembrance Day, in November 2017.

## The parable of the talents (Matthew 25:14–30), Mike Holroyd

First, a question: Who are you? Who am I? Or perhaps, who do I think you are? And who do you think I am? Or, if we want to get down to the essential question: who do you think I think that you are? We have many identities and characteristics that make up who we are; things like age, sexuality, gender, race, economic background, etc. But we can also develop an identity through what we think other people are thinking about us – I am not who I am, I am not who you think I am: I am who I think you think I am ...

I always feel very sorry for the third person in the parable – he is afraid and fearful, yet he seems to be judged most harshly. I think the key here is our perception of God. The first two players in the parable seemed to have an idea of God as kind, caring, loving, forgiving and so on. They were able to take risks because they knew a deep sense of peace and security. The third player's problems start not with the burial of the treasure, but with the perception of God: 'I know you reap where you do not sow ...' A limited view of God as harsh and judgemental always generates fear and insecurity. With this there is no desire to take risks: we cling on to what we have without any desire to explore or even trust others with our treasures. This leads to a profound sense of self-judgement, where we see ourselves as never good enough, never able to take risks, never able to step out of a very limited sense of security. The judgement is not God's judgement, but our own judgement of ourselves. Even the sense of self-worth and dignity that we had becomes eroded to nothing as we judge ourselves more and more harshly.

I yearn for the day when, at our service for Transgender Remembrance Day, there are no longer 304 names on the screen of people who have lost their lives, but no names at all. I yearn for the day when we can live without fear of prejudice and ignorance. Why, in 2017, are people still being killed and victimised for who God has created them to be? A limited view of God, or even a limited view of how society should be, impacts not only on our own self-judgement but also on the way in which we judge others. Transgender Remembrance interprets the parable for us – a view of God or society as generous, kind and caring enables all our talents to flourish, including the exploration of our gender identities. We all have a role to play in celebrating and promoting the virtues of kindness, compassion, openness and so on. We need gently to take by the hand those who seek to bury our treasures, and lead them into a place of risk and growth, built on a foundation of peace and security in a God whose very nature is love. As Christians, we need to confess a history of intolerance, and be prepared to lead the way forward in creating a society where no one's life is lost because of who they are or what they believe.

You may be wondering why the person preaching this sermon is not someone who identifies as transgender – I identify as gay. Sometimes we need to hear others speak up and speak out on our behalf. Sometimes we become tired and disheartened and we need to know that people who do not directly share our experience are willing to speak up and speak out for us. This is something we can all do for each other – this is what it means to be a truly inclusive community – my issue is your issue, my struggle is your struggle, my celebration is your celebration.

So, let us allow our ever-expanding vision of God to enable us to live in a spirit of generosity and compassion. Let us speak up and speak out for one another, and let us do all we can to eliminate the fearful view of God that leads to judgement and death.

*We are a people of hope;*
*let us share that hope with all people.*
*Amen*

Social and political action

Social and political action can take many forms, from writing to our MP to supporting organisations campaigning for change. Sometimes, it can also involve more radical action.

Norman Shanks wrote to me, telling more about his work:

## Action, Norman Shanks

Both as Convener of the Church of Scotland's Church and Nation Committee (1988-92) and as Leader of the Iona Community (1995-2002), there were continuing and frequent opportunities for media involvement, interaction with a range of other organisations, speaking at and attending conferences, meetings and demonstrations around justice and peace issues and themes (Stop the War, closure of the Ravenscraig steelworks, climate change, Make Poverty History, nuclear disarmament, etc). I joined the Labour Party in 1992/3 but resigned after little more than two years over the issue of Purchasing Power Parity (PPP) and the Private Finance Initiative (PFI) and I have felt insufficiently drawn since then to any particular party to take the step of becoming a member.

More specifically, among many highlights over the years, in October 1990 I took part in a visit to Israel/Palestine by 'Scottish church leaders' and a further Church of Scotland visit in May 2017 – both thoroughly memorable experiences – that made a deep and lasting impression on me; and I am currently a member of the Community's Concern Network on Palestine/Israel.

In the 1990s, while lecturing at Glasgow University, I was caught up in discussions about human sexuality, gay rights and the debate on Clause 28, which stated that a local authority *'shall not intentionally promote homosexuality or publish material with the intention of promoting homosexuality'* or *'promote the teaching in any maintained school of the acceptability of homosexuality as a pretended family rela-*

*tionship'*. I was a member of the first of several Church of Scotland special working groups on this issue (which in 1994 presented a report that was too radical for the General Assembly) and well remember appearing in a live BBC Scotland TV debate, chaired by Kirsty Wark before she graduated to *Newsnight*. This was a challenging, at times uncomfortable, experience; it was interesting, even amusing, to find myself on the opposite side to some vociferous representatives of conservative Christian groups and on the same side as prominent gay activists and a leading conservative politician, who was a Kirk elder with liberal views and later leader of the Tories in the Scottish Parliament – with whom I had crossed swords in public several times before on 'political' issues!

I have regarded my membership of and commitment to church, ecumenical and other committees as an effective and valid expression of my commitment to keeping and living by the Community's Rule. My role as Church and Nation Committee Convener involved high-profile engagement with a range of social and political issues during the Thatcher years and beyond, interaction with government, political parties and third sector bodies, and frequent (sometimes daily) media requests for comments or appearances. I was a member of the European Ecumenical Commission on Church and Society from 1990-95; this was the Protestant Churches' link with the European Union institutions and is now part of the Conference of European Churches. From 1988-97, as a representative of the churches, I was a member of the Scottish Constitutional Convention that laid the foundations for the Scottish Parliament. I was also a member of the Board of Christian Aid (2000-04); Convener of the ecumenical body Action of Churches Together (ACTS) Commission on Justice, Peace, Social and Moral Issues (1992–95); and a member of the Central Committee of the World Council of Churches (1998–2006), at whose meetings and Assemblies (Harare 2008, Porto Alegre 2006) justice and peace issues frequently figured on the agenda.

Sometimes radical action is necessary to obtain justice. One of the major themes for Community action has been opposition to nuclear weapons. We are willing to stand up for our views, and to bear the consequences. Protests have regularly taken place at the Trident base at Faslane.

Brian Quail, a member from Glasgow, writes:

## Nuclear weapons, Brian Quail

Andrei Sakharov, Nobel prize-winning physicist and 'father' of the Soviet H-bomb, said, *'The struggle against nuclear war must take precedence over every other human interest and activity.'*[1] He said this, because it threatens to cause universal death.

Irrespective of the unimaginable human carnage it promises, it means environmental suicide. Even a small-scale war would cause a nuclear winter and, in effect, sterilise the planet.

Trident has this capability. In my view, it is the ultimate evil. It is the worst thing in the world. And we are willing to use it.

Many members of the Community have campaigned and demonstrated against Trident. Member Molly Harvey is retired and lives in Glasgow. In 2001 she was arrested with fellow members for taking part in a communion service and then sitting in the road outside Faslane, and was taken to Cornton Vale prison for women. Molly had visited folk in Cornton Vale when she was Coordinator of Glasgow Braendam Link, a grassroots organisation which supports families living in poverty.

# (Put) away for the weekend, Molly Harvey

Faslane, 2001, found me sitting on the road, and thereby breaking the law. It is not how I would necessarily have chosen to spend a day in February, nor was it something I had undertaken lightly. In fact, I firmly believed that I had no choice in the matter, for two reasons:

*1. Trident is capable of destroying most of the northern hemisphere in 10 minutes. Thirty million men, women and children would be wiped out, and the effect of radiation would make much of the Earth uninhabitable. I would therefore be failing my children and my grandchildren if I did not make a stand against it.*

*2. The cost of Trident in 2001 was said to be the equivalent of spending £30,000 a day since the birth of Christ. Is this what we, a so-called civilised society, really consider to be a responsible use of money? At the time, I worked in partnership with families living in poverty and social exclusion in Glasgow, and felt I would be failing these people, whom I feel privileged to call my friends, if I did not make a stand against such obscene expenditure.*

I was found guilty of *'breach of the peace and conducting myself in a disorderly manner'* (taking part in a communion service and then sitting on the road).

*15th March, 2002:*

I was summoned to appear at Means Enquiry Court in Glasgow as I had failed to pay the fine of £150 incurred as a result of the breach of the peace. A family friend phoned and told me she had taken money out of her savings account and would bring it to the court. 'I don't want you going to Cornton Vale,' she said (she'd spent a considerable part of her life there). I was very touched but explained I was doing it as a matter of principle.

In court I was very nervous but managed to speak:

*Molly:*       *The non-payment of my fine is a continuation of my protest (peaceful and non-violent) against the British Government's possession of nuclear weapons.*

*Response:*   *I take it you are not interested in a Supervised Attendance Order?*

*Molly:*       *I am very interested in it, but would find it extremely difficult in terms of my work and other commitments.*

*Response:*   *You realise I have no alternative but to send you to prison?*

*Molly:*       *Yes, and I'm prepared to accept the consequences of my action.*

*Response:*   *Seven days in Cornton Vale prison.*

An officer took me out. 'What did you go and do that for?' she said. 'I'm sorry, I'm going to have to lock you in.' I felt a sense of relief – at least that bit, the bit I was nervous about, was over, and now it was just a case of going with the flow. I settled down with a new Joanna Trollope book.

I did not have long to read though. 'We're going to transfer you over to Turnbull Street. Are you going to give me any grief?' said an officer. 'No, not at all.' 'Well, I'll not put you in handcuffs. Are you a teacher or something? I can see you're an educated woman.'

So, I travelled in the back of the police van with two officers, all shut in. At Turnbull Street, I was searched and all my property examined by a wee woman officer (who could have been your granny): 'I'm really sorry, hen, to have to do this, I don't like doing this at all.' The cell included a loo, a mouldy bed on the floor and a single wooden bench. However, I had the book, the *Herald* and my specs. 'I'll just get you a wee cup of tea,' the officer told me.

Soon I was taken, handcuffed this time, with apologies, to the Sheriff Court, again with two officers: 'Just sit up at the front and we'll open the grille – sorry about the mess in here … Just watch yourself and keep your head down and you'll be all right.' Over the river we went, into Gorbals and South Portland Street. I was reminded of campaigning in the 1960s, and felt almost excited!

Because the steel shutters of the garage and the van door stuck, I had to get out of the front – not easy with the handcuffs on – and from there into a cage. It was about the size of a small bathroom, with a wooden bench on either side, a water fountain in the back wall and a grille in the front. I still had the book and the *Herald* but by this time had no glasses or watch.

My grille looked out onto a counter and into an office. To the right were the locked doors of the women's section. I could see beyond that to the main reception counter, where there was a lot of coming and going. Men's cages to the right. I could not see the men, but could hear a constant stream of Glasgow patter, effing and blinding, yelling, shouting and drunken roaring. After an hour or so, I got up to stretch and realised that I could see a clock above the counter. I asked if there was a chance of having my glasses and these eventually came (minus the chain) so I settled down with my book. After a couple of hours, I felt really hungry so asked about food. I was told that I'd had my lunch, and a voice came from the cage next door: 'Naw, that lassie never came in till after the lunches.' I was told that we'd get a sandwich before we went up to Cornton Vale.

All afternoon there was a great scurrying of lawyers hither and thither, with names being yelled out for court appearance, one of which I knew but wasn't able to see. At 4.30pm a packet of sandwiches was offered, fairly bland and insipid turkey salad – but delicious, plus a packet of three Bourbon biscuits and a cup of tea. I was taken to the toilet handcuffed to two women from the next cage, who looked spaced out on drugs, which made me a bit apprehensive, then back into the prison van. That journey was the scariest bit of the whole experience as the van was travelling at speed, with the male driver showing off to the female officer. 'Let's get up this road!' I remember thinking: *If this van turns over and sets on fire and we're handcuffed, how will we get out? Or will the steel prevent the fire, and we will melt to death? My family will be so angry with me for putting my life at risk like this.*

It was with relief that we arrived at the jail and were taken to a cubicle with a clear explanation of exactly what would happen next. I was issued with a clean (although not white and fluffy) towel and bathrobe and asked to strip. I was searched, had a shower on my own and went back to the cubicle, where a pile of clothes was waiting: T-shirt (green), sweatshirt (grey), trousers (black), three pairs of new flowery knickers and socks (two pairs, white).

I was then seen by the nurse and asked about any problems, or medication I had been prescribed, and a male officer asked me whether I had any concerns or anxieties, and whether I might be likely to commit suicide. Back at the desk my property was processed. I was allowed my own underwear but not slipper socks. Allowed my book, folder of work and other papers, two biros, but not my spiral notebook and not my spiral Pilates book (I had thought I might get time for exercise). My facecloth was OK, but no other toiletries or paper hankies. My wee stock of apples, lemon-and-ginger teabags and Disprin was not allowed. I kept my wedding ring and watch, glasses (and the chain) but not my engagement ring or earrings. Cash was counted, £11.84, of which I spent £6 on three phonecards stamped with HMP Cornton Vale. Everything else was signed for and locked up.

I was taken to the 'Younger Unit', which seemed quite tatty and rundown. I was told very little apart from how to phone home, given a pint of milk and a packet of teabags, and shown to my cell (Y36). Bunk beds down one side, countertop down the other with handbasin at the end. There was a TV, a small kettle and two blue plastic mugs and spoons. The 'welcome pack' included toothbrush and paste, shampoo, a comb and soap. I was shown the emergency button. I chose the top bunk. I was anxious about who may be sharing with me, and very pleased when B arrived (37!) from Dundee. We chatted a bit. She'd been arrested in her house at one in the morning for non-payment of a fine/community service and had spent the day in Bell Street police station. She was very worried about her sons, who were 12 and 13, and her daughter, who was 16 and had just discovered she was pregnant.

I asked for another chair, and was told to go and get one out of the 'dining room'. I also asked what we did if we needed the loo in the night, and was taken to get a supply of hospital potties. The officer told me that 'some girls just use the sink'. I used to think, when I was living in the Gorbals Group, that you got very close to folk if you were all sharing your money, but you do, too, if you share a sink to pee in – and then to clean your teeth. What happens, I thought, if you needed more than a pee? What about heavy periods, etc?

I was asleep by 10.30, whilst my roommate watched some telly. I slept really well. We were unlocked at about 9am; fortunately I hadn't needed the loo, although my roommate had!

The weekend was much the same, except on Sunday we were asked if anyone wanted to go to church, but I was in the toast queue at the time, which was fairly important, so I didn't make it. We had breakfast around tables that sat about eight. Cornflakes and bran flakes but as there were no bowls, I used an extra mug. There was a container of blackcurrant juice, which made a change to the endless tea. There were little packets of jam, but no plates, but we could take these back to the cell. There was a queue for medication – my Disprin had not arrived! Meals and medication queues were the point of contact with the rest of the unit, which housed between 30 and 40 women. Several asked what I was in for and were familiar with nuclear protestors. (An officer told me we were known as 'tree huggers'.)

An attractive young girl told me that she was a doctor's daughter and was in on 25 drugs-related charges. She was desperate to get off drugs, and had been in and out of prison.

We were supposed to be told what kind of cleaning we were to do, but nobody told us – fine!

Lunch was hamburger, chips and beans; another day, baked potato, coleslaw and salad. We were 'dubbed up' (locked up) for over an hour after lunch – siesta time, which was great as we watched the afternoon film (I don't think I have ever done that before). Helen Steven and Ellen Moxley, both Iona Community members, and Stirling CND sent me beautiful flowers – my roommate: 'Ya spoi-elt bitch.' And later, to others: 'We've got floo-ers – we've arraived!'

Tea was steak pie, or tuna pasta with cabbage and tatties, plus goodies for the night (dubbed up early at weekends, 7pm). The goodies consisted of sandwiches, an apple and a sachet of hot chocolate (I had been fantasising about fruit and chocolate). Another night it was ham and pineapple and potatoes and a tub of ice cream, plus a sachet of coffee for a treat.

We got ourselves into a routine for the nights. One day we saw one of the officers coming in with some newspapers, so we yelled out asking to look at them. We could really plan the telly then!

Time passed amazingly quickly. My roommate wrote a long letter to her family, which I said I would post when I got out – she was grateful for some paper and a spare biro. I tried to write down as much as I could remember, read a couple of work papers and finished my Joanna Trollope book. Outside exercise was offered each day. I phoned my husband, John, who was finding it hard, me being inside. It was probably much harder for him because he just had to sit and imagine it, plus he was off sick at the time.

My roommate and I wondered what had happened to a woman

who had been in such a state when she came in that she had been put on high watch. An officer asked if the woman could come and sit with us for a bit, and after that she was with us most of the time. She was in a cell on her own next door to us, and would move into my bed when I left the next day.

When the cell doors were open, people tended to drop in to see one another. One of our neighbours was in for beating up a policeman, another had spat in a policeman's eye during a fight – she had just had a miscarriage, and her baby had died from cot death just 12 months earlier. One, who had a black eye, was in for nine years following the death of her two-year-old child, who had died from neglect and starvation whilst she and her partner, both drug users, had supposedly left him locked in a room and fed him cornflakes and temazepam through the letterbox. We were asked by others why we had let her in our room; we responded 'we are new here'.

Everybody smoked. I didn't see anyone who did not. If I had been there longer, I think I may have asked about the possibility of a non-smoking cell, but who you shared a cell with seemed much more important. I got on really well with my roommate, and that made all the difference to my short stay. She said that I'd made it much easier for her too, 'and you never judged me for being on drugs'. She told me that she was in for carrying a blade (she had taken it off a mate in case he got caught with it) and for shoplifting. She longed to be free of drugs and the lifestyle and people it involved her with. She was put on a detox programme. She longed to be able to move from the very bad area of Dundee where she stayed, back to where her father still lived. Her mother and a couple of close aunts had all died a few years previously. She explained that she had been in a relationship with a younger man recently, but had finished with him as she did not feel good enough for him and was scared that she'd 'drag him down'.

We were both in tears when I left on Monday morning. Liberation day came. About 9am I was taken to reception and all my belongings were returned. I was given a travel warrant for the train to Glasgow. YES!

Helen and Ellen had phoned John and insisted they meet me and take me for breakfast – other Community members had also offered. Ellen was in the waiting room, a space I remembered well from coming to meet folk from Braendam Link. She said that Helen was waiting for us at home. I explained that I needed to get back to Glasgow to John and the grandchildren (who I was due to be baby-sitting). So Ellen took me to Bridge of Allan for a delicious breakfast and caffè lattes, then on to Stirling Station.

I felt as high as a kite. Freedom. I was glad to have done it, but so excited to be going home.

Sally Beaumont, a member from Glasgow, writes:

## A day at the lochside, Sally Beaumont

*07.00, 23 August 2004*

A familiar early-morning sight – the loch calm and beautiful, the hills opposite, green and rolling, the north gate closed, colourful figures milling about – too many to count – yellow-clad police standing in a circle. Faslane again. The site of our Trident submarines, our weapons of mass destruction. The Greens were there, the SSP were there, Trident Ploughshares were there, Clergy for Peace were there, among many others, protesting against WMD.

The Adomnán of Iona Affinity Group, a branch of Trident Ploughshares, were there, trying to hand in a letter to the Commodore of the base. We had told her we were coming but she did not come. Undeterred, we sat down in the road to wait.

Two hours later, in a police cell in Clydebank, I slept for a while. The clanging door awoke me and two women entered. We exchanged first names, and talked of the blockade. Several minutes later the warder appeared at the grille, and said: 'You two, your press officer wants to know if you are okay?' Answer from them: 'Fine.'

'Who are you two?' I asked.

Two members of the Scottish Parliament, they said.

Two MSPs in a cell with a white-haired OAP. This could be interesting, I thought.

Shut up in a cell together for five hours, we had the time and quiet to exchange stories. Sharing a cell provides an extraordinary ambience, if there is sensitivity and a will to listen. The stories were not always hilarious, but often so. Sometimes the stories inspired thought and reflection. R shared stories of her feelings of respect and delight at meeting the Dalai Lama. F shared the story of her beloved son starting school. I shared the story of my evacuation to Canada during World War Two. R exclaimed, 'I've never met anyone who was evacuated!' And so it went on.

We also talked about our reasons for being there – our abhorrence of nuclear weapons, the obscenity and immorality of them. It reminded me of a part of a letter sent to me by friends in the States:

*'When you've just gotten your butt kicked again, and it doesn't make sense to drag yourself out of bed, I think of some words of Phil Ochs:*

*"It is wrong to expect a reward for your struggles. The reward is the act of struggle itself, not what you win. Even though you can't expect to defeat the absurdity of the world, you must make that attempt. That's morality, that's religion. That's art. That's life."'* [2]

Later that night we emerged into the rain (my son-in-law had come to collect me) and I bade a fond farewell to my new friends. I will not always agree with them, they will not always agree with me, but for a few hours we had listened and laughed and shared together.

Member Brian Quail made the national newspaper headlines in 2017:

*[Photo caption:] A pensioner who single-handedly stopped a nuclear convoy by sitting in the middle of the road has arrived at court.*

*[Report:] Brian Quail, 78, appeared at court in Dumbarton, yesterday charged with breach of the peace.*

*In March last year, Quail brought a convoy of four lorries to a grinding halt after flagging them down at a roundabout in Balloch, also West Dunbartonshire.*

*He pleaded not guilty and plans to represent himself.*

*Quail was flanked by several other anti-nuclear campaigners from the Campaign for Nuclear Disarmament upon his arrival at Dumbarton Sheriff Court.*

*The retired classics teacher has 14 previous convictions for similar offences and has been in jail for failing to pay his fine five times.*

*Ahead of the court date, he said: 'Trident is the worst thing in the world. The epitome of evil. I do infinitesimally small things against it, because that is all I can do. But consent by silence or inactivity I cannot give.'*

*The trial continues.*

Metro, 25 January, 2017 [3]

A visitor to Iona once asked me why some Community members risk so much in confronting issues that do not affect them 'personally'. At the time, I found the question difficult to answer. Brian Quail, in a closing speech at an earlier court case, says this:

... Let me finish on a personal note. Several years ago I had heart surgery – a double bypass.

This was at the time when Trident warheads were first being sent up to Scotland from Burghfield in Berkshire.

The good folk of Faslane Peace Camp, John Ainslie the administrator of SCND and I used to regularly follow these convoys and hold them up whenever we could safely do so. I had noticed that every time I saw them and heard the particular roar of the Foden carriers, I would get intense chest pains. This got worse and worse; until finally things came to a head on one occasion when we stopped the convoy at the roundabout up from the north gate of Faslane. The lead vehicle was stopped and I ran up to support the action. The pains grew more and more intense. I collapsed on the road in agony. People crowded round and someone said, 'We'll need to take him to the hospital.'

I said, 'No, leave me here.'

The pains were unbearable, like tiger's claws in my chest. I thought: *This is it. I am dying. Why am I dying here, on the road beside a vehicle carrying nuclear bombs?*

I looked up at a patch of blue in the sky, and it reminded me of my youngest daughter Catherine, who has particularly lovely blue eyes. Then I thought, *No, it's not just the blue eyes of my children, but the green eyes, and the brown eyes, and the grey eyes of all the children of the world – and their mothers and fathers too – that are the target of our bombs. Our fellow human beings, our brothers and sisters, whom we are prepared to burn and blast.*

And I knew the answer to my question 'why here?' It is love that drives me. Love is not an emotional or sentimental feeling. Active love is a harsh and fearful thing.

So I am not a peace protestor, I am – though I don't look it – a lover.[4]

Nuclear weapons are indeed immoral. Fighting violence with violence destructive. In a world where war is never far away, peace, and how we achieve it, is a challenge and a burning passion for many of us, from all walks of life. The late Helen Steven, a former Iona Community Justice and Peace Worker, wrote:

History has shown time and again that justice won by violent means already sows the deadly seeds of the next conflict. When I worked in Vietnam, my sympathies were almost entirely with the North Vietnamese revolutionary struggle, and it seemed that the quickest way to achieve justice for the suffering Vietnamese was for the North Vietnamese to win the war as quickly as possible. Which is what, ultimately, they did, but, although the immediate prospect of peace was welcome, already, a new powerful group was oppressing, killing, torturing, and the cycle of violence and injustice remained unbroken.

This is where, I believe, non-violence can provide a way forward. I totally agree that non-violence which allows violating to go on is a form of violence itself – in fact, it is not non-violence. The very essence of non-violence is that it resists and opposes all forms of injustice and oppression to the last drop of its blood. It can never consent to anything that degrades the human spirit.

Non-violence is about revolution. It is about finding creative, imaginative ways to overthrow all forms of tyranny and oppression, without becoming the oppressor in the process. It widens the options and holds out a possibility of a way out of the cycle of violence where dignity can be maintained.[5]

## Prayer

*Empower us to continue to stand up for what is right,*
*what is just,*
*and to fight always for the rights of others.*
*Amen*

Susan Dale

## Sources and notes

1. Source unknown

2. From *The Complete Phil Ochs: Chords of Fame*, 1978, Almo Publications. And frequently quoted on the Internet.

3. From the *Metro*: http://metro.co.uk/2017/01/25/pensioner-who-single-handedly-stopped-a-nuclear-convoy-appears-in-court-6405821/ #ixzz4nTiuXzPU

4. From www.autonomyscotland.org/brian-quails-anti-trident-court-speech

5. From 'An idea whose time has come', by Helen Steven, *Coracle*, the magazine of the Iona Community, 2008, Neil Paynter (Ed.)

The Poverty Truth Commission

The divide between rich and poor is more marked today than ever.

Although we are the world's sixth richest country, the Social Metrics Commission, in 2019, reported that there were '*14.3 million people in poverty in the UK. This includes 8.3 million working-age adults; 4.6 million children; and 1.3 million pension-age adults*'.[1]

At the time of writing, we have not yet had the statistics for 2020, which currently faces a tsunami of additional people in poverty following the Covid-19 crisis and expected recession.

I spoke with John Harvey, a former Iona Community Leader, and Christine Jones, who is a Methodist minister and Community member living in Cheshire, about the difficulties of poverty, and how this is being addressed where they live.

## Conversations about the birth of the Poverty Truth Commission, John Harvey

I think it was about 10 years ago, when I heard about this chap called Paul Chapman – who was a 70-year-old man from the U.S. who was working in new ways to solve poverty.

Martin Johnstone, whom I knew, and who was then working for the Faith in Community Scotland project, managed to persuade Paul to come to Scotland and talk with us.

Paul came over to Scotland to talk with us and to work on what later became called the Poverty Truth Commission.

Paul was asked, because he had experience in the States of setting up similar projects.

I think he got his inspiration for the Poverty Truth Commission work partly from South Africa, where they had a Truth and Reconciliation

Commission. It was also partly from the people of New Orleans, who after Hurricane Katrina had banded together because they did not want to be subjected to any of this …

'drop-down' aid.

Aid that was being thrust upon them by central government.

The government was trying to tell them how they were going to rebuild their own city, and … they wanted a say in how that city needed to be rebuilt.

So, they ganged up together under this marvellous slogan, which had been used in the anti-apartheid movement in South Africa:

*'Nothing about us, without us, is for us.'*

So, Paul came, and Molly (my wife) and I were asked to gather a few people together. Molly had in the past worked with the Glasgow Braendam Link, which was set up to work alongside families in poverty.

Molly ran the project for a while, so had good connections with people who had experience of living with poverty.

We were asked to gather at our house in Glasgow, where Paul would come and explain his plan. And that's what happened.

There was a bit of a difficulty understanding each other …

Paul's American accent mixed with the group's Glasgow accents … all that stuff was quite tricky. But eventually people got the hang of it.

Some of these folk were to be what at that time were called 'testifiers'. They were going to work on telling their stories of living with poverty.

They were going to get some help with how best to do that – either by speaking their stories, or by writing them ... or by dramatising them, or in one case, someone used puppets to tell their story.

Various ways to tell the stories of poverty.

Telling of what it was like to live with poverty.

Eventually, after a couple of years of preparation, there was a big public meeting in Glasgow City Chambers. Right in the centre of the city.

We invited people, who at that time we called 'commissioners'.

These were people from various walks of life; they could be considered powerful people. People like journalists from TV, the churches, from politics and from the Scottish Government.

Important people.

There must have been about 12, or even 15 of them.

The moderator of the General Assembly,
the Archbishop of Glasgow,
and so on, and so on ...

And what happened at that meeting – and the hall was filled to capacity, two to three thousand people, in this huge banqueting hall.

What happened, was that the testifiers ...
I cannot remember how many there were ...
they came and told their stories,
and the commissioners listened ... or watched.

And then the commissioners were invited to go away into a separate room, and work on their response to what they'd heard.

The crucial thing that really all made the thing take off, was when they came back after half an hour ...

perhaps three quarters of an hour, and spoke.

They didn't say:

'that was very moving, we've heard what you've had to say, and we'll certainly try and do something about it'.

What they said in effect was:

'we'd like to meet with you', and that opened the door.

Suddenly there was a real opportunity for conversation between the folk who were the real experts on poverty – those who were living in it – and the folk who could do something about it. And they wanted to do it 'with them', together and ...

*'Nothing about us, without us, is for us.'*

And, as Martin Johnstone said at the end of that particular meeting,

'You know ...

if the struggle for civil rights, in the south of the USA, had been led by well-meaning white liberals, it would have got nowhere.

But because it was led by the people, people who were suffering from the results of racial segregation, and the white liberals were prepared to come and work with them, rather than do it for them, that made a difference.'

So,

that is where the Poverty Truth Commission in Scotland sprang up from; and then what happened was that everybody then became called commissioners; they stopped having testifiers and commissioners, they were all commissioners. Part of the Poverty Truth Commission.

Initially they set up three working groups; from memory, I think, one was on media issues, one was on knife crime and the other was on kinship caring.

And evidence was taken from all of these three groups. The media group, for instance, looked at how to get the media to stop presenting poverty in a bad light.

And knife crime ...

one of the original commissioners on this group was John Carnochan, who was at that point head of the Violence Reduction Unit of Glasgow with the Strathclyde Police, and he openly says his life was changed ...

changed by hearing stories from these people who were suffering from knife crime and so on.

And then it took off.

It's still going, and they work on a three-year rolling programme. Every three years the commissioners change and the projects change. And they make their report, and then new working groups are formed. [2]

## Conversations about the birth of the Poverty Truth Commission, Christine Jones with John Harvey

*Chris:*

While I was an associate member and really learning about the Iona Community, I bought a book, this is maybe 15-20 years ago. A book edited by Kathy Galloway called *Starting Where We Are* [Wild Goose Publications]. It was the story of a neighbourhood centre in Orbiston, near Glasgow, and Martin Johnstone was the facilitator of that piece of work.

Kathy told the story of it – and it really caught my imagination. It was hugely influential, really, in me getting caught up more in the Iona Community, and I went quite a few times to meet Martin and see the work in Orbiston. And a lot of the work I did in Ellesmere Port, with the church there, was largely using his kind of thinking …

We took this approach:

Reading the Bible, and asking, 'What is this saying to us?' We did this throughout our journey.

So, if you like, I connected with Martin's ministry and I knew through John about this Poverty Truth Commission work, because I would hear it discussed within the Iona Community meetings.

Our dispersed Community has so many people working on these kinds of issues, and that has massive implications, huge resources really.

I was always sort of tuning into what was happening, and just before the 2015 general election, the Archbishop of Canterbury produced a leaflet, through the ecumenical Joint Public Issues Team, and they held an event that was called 'Think, Pray, Vote' and the Archbishop of Canterbury was the speaker and Martin Johnstone was doing a workshop.

It was in Birmingham, and a friend, Rose, and I decided we were going to go and listen to Martin Johnstone.

So, we went to this event, and Martin told us there that the Poverty Truth Commission had been awarded some funding through the Joseph Rowntree Foundation to cascade the methodology across the UK.

We said to him there and then:

'We would really like to be able to do this where we live, but we don't know how yet, but we are going to go away, knowing what you told us.'

So we went away ... and a little bit later ...

I am involved with West Cheshire Food Bank, so is Rose, and our council, the full council, were having a council debate about why we needed a food bank.

As trustees, Rose and I went, but we weren't allowed to participate; we stood on the side and listened while they debated, and the outcome of this debate was that there was an agreement that there was to be a cross-party working group on poverty.

So, we knew then that we had our opportunity. We made an appointment to go and see the councillors and told them how we had heard about the working group.

We asked them to consider whether this was an opportunity for a Poverty Truth Commission and whether they would consider adopting that as a way of working.

They said that they would consider the matter ...

They wanted to go away and find out a bit more. Martin Johnstone sent us some initial papers, which we were able to give to them, and to be honest ...

we left it to them ...

because we knew we had to do that. Eventually, they invited Martin to come to Chester; he came, and we had our first meeting.

And since then they've been totally committed to it. It's been a cross-party initiative. They've had the Lord Lieutenant, David Briggs, who is Chair of West Cheshire PTC ...

and he's been totally committed to it, and he's been to every meeting we've ever had.

I think they'd be the first people to say that they've really struggled at times ...

The council offered meetings at the council offices, sitting round tables, and it was really difficult ...

so, so difficult,

because they wanted to arrange ... organise everything.

The council asking questions such as, 'Who should we invite?'

'We don't know yet, because actually, the people living with poverty need to decide for themselves what the issues are. We cannot assume things ...'

And then, the most amazing breakthrough was when ...

I knew that we had to get them to Glasgow, get them in a situation where they could see the Commission in action ...

In the beginning, it was frustrating.

It changed when we went to Glasgow though. That was just amazing.

I will never forget that day.

Martin had invited some of the commissioners from Glasgow – by this stage they had had years of experience. It was the Kinship Care Group commissioners, and there was no arguing with how well the process worked.

The people from Cheshire West were totally convinced by the story of the kinship carers.

Because ...

they had managed to change government policy.

The kinship carers were looking after their own family members; these would often be grandchildren, or nieces and nephews, and the missing generation – the parents – were either in prison or had addiction problems or those sort of issues.

So essentially it was the grandparents, really, who were bringing up the children. They were looking after little ones, and in a lot of the cases, on a pension with no additional funding.

They never asked for funding for themselves, but they did want their children to have the same sort of opportunities as other children,

which they didn't have …

Because in most cases the grandparents weren't working, they didn't have the same sort of resources as a parent might have.

Scottish legislation has changed because of the work of the Poverty Truth Commission, and now there is a significant amount of money every year allocated for these children.

It had a massive impact at a national level.

Before the Commission started, support for this group was a bit patchy …

it was not a level playing field for these children.

That was the start of it really, for me, for the people in West Cheshire 'getting it'.

We met some amazing people that day in Glasgow, including a quiet, poised woman …

I will never forget her, as long as I live …

My goodness, she spoke so well.

She was one of the original testifying commissioners when the process had started in Glasgow, she and her daughter.

She was just an amazing woman.

The testifiers now work at the Scottish Government level, mentoring civil servants and politicians.

On the day we went to Glasgow, what was really noticeable was that when we got there, we were all given a drink, as Martin was very keen that we did not start until everybody was there, so ...

Somebody had been held up on the way and the councillors ... they became quite agitated – because it was past the time we should have started.

But anyway, Martin held out and we waited for this person to arrive, and then when he came, Martin said, 'We will start how we usually do.

I want you to introduce yourselves ...

first names only, no titles, we leave those at the door, and I want you to tell us what you had for your tea last night.'

And the impact of that simple introduction, it was such a leveller, it was just amazing.

And I think the councillors themselves were great.

They were lovely, and great trust has grown; taking off their lanyards though and leaving those aside was really, really hard for them and when they agreed the agenda ...

they agreed what they were going to talk about actually at the meeting, and they put it on large pieces of paper and put it in the centre, on the floor, so that you hadn't got an agenda that somebody else had produced in advance.

It is an agenda that is agreed at the start of the meeting among the people there.

As we dealt with each thing, we picked up the sheet and somebody wrote notes on it.

The whole thing was owned by everybody …

people started telling their stories immediately.

*John:*

The important people spoke first …

such as those living with the challenges of being a kinship carer.

It was very difficult in Glasgow, at the beginning, for the councillors and others to move out of their comfort zone of: agendas, papers, pencils, order of meetings. But it took only two meetings for the other people to say:

'Sorry, we're not coming back unless you change that.'

They said:

'We're not going to come and sit at a desk and talk when we're told to talk. We don't do it that way.

That's not the way we want to work.'

So, the councillors had to give up their desks, and their pens, and their microphones, and sit together on the floor – just like here on Iona.

Molly's group used to come up to Iona when we were leaders there, and they said: 'When we're on Iona the labels are off … It's Molly and John and a common humanity, and that really works very well.'

*Chris:*

And I think what I have seen is that someone said to me, 'But this is against the way of a council working to do it like this' … but it works!

We've now got Edgehill University involved as well.

We've now got an academic institution involved.

I see that as a good thing, because what they're doing … They are acting as outside eyes and they're reflecting on the journey this council has made.

We're really making some progress now. All 50 commissioners have now met together for their first meeting.

People are saying: however hard it has been so far, even just to have that one meeting, it has been worth it!

In Chester, Chester racecourse, which is a big prestigious place, they have given us that racecourse for the launch.

For anyone interested, there is a YouTube clip about Cheshire Poverty Truth Commission.[3]

It's about four minutes long and it's a little cartoon that explains what a Poverty Truth Commission is.

It's really, really good.

It's about changing attitudes …

I know ...
that even though I am the one
who has been working with Chester, here in this Community,
there are members who understand,
and who you can go to,
and you can listen to,
or be inspired by ...

and I think that's a strength for me.

I mean that I know buildings such as the Iona Centres are an important part of the Community because they are a gathering space ...

but it's the nature of the Community that feels important to me.

*John:*

The power of stories ...

We persuaded Harriet Harman
(who was then the Secretary of State for Social Security) to come to Glasgow, with her civil servants, to listen in the meetings to the folks living with poverty.
She said she would only come if there was no media presence.

And she came, and it was chaired entirely by the folk, and they just told their stories, and she and her civil servants were made to listen (whether they wanted to or not), and as a result of that, the department produced new guidelines for people working in the benefit offices.

And, of course, it is not a 'one-off' thing.

This has to be done each generation; people seem to be programmed ...

for those in power not to always do things in the most helpful way.

*Sue:*

We often 'do things for people' instead of empowering them to do it for themselves.

*Chris:*

It's been important to remember that it has changed so much … our work through the food bank, for example …

When we started it, it was very transactional – you come here with a voucher because you need emergency food, you give us the voucher, and then we will give you food. We're moving now, instead, to develop places of welcome. It's much more relational, and not so transactional.

*Sue:*

That has to be good?

*Chris:*

It is, but I think that the journey with the Poverty Truth Commission has helped to shape what will eventually happen.

And we are just writing a development plan, which has got a time-line that says …
'by 2020 this food bank will not exist any more'
that's because hopefully we have developed these places of welcome.

We've learned what it means to be a catalyst for people, and that's been a very important lesson.

**Prayer**

*Listen with me, Lord,*
*at this time, in this space, with this person.*
*Help me to hear both the words that are spoken,*
*and those that are not.*

*Speak through me, Lord,*
*at this time, in this space, with this person.*
*Help me to find the words that enable,*
*rather than those that disable.*

*Stand with me, Lord,*
*at this time, in this space, with this person.*
*Help me to find the strength to stand alongside,*
*when all within me is trembling and fearful.*

*See with me, Lord,*
*at this time, in this space, with this person.*
*Help me to see your face in their face,*
*your view of them rather than my own.*

*Be with me, Lord,*
*at this time, in this space. Amen* [4]

Susan Dale

## Sources and notes

1. From *Measuring Poverty 2019: A Report of the Social Metrics Commission*. Chaired by Philippa Stroud, CEO of the Legatum Institute, July 2019. Report available at: https://socialmetricscommission.org.uk

2. The Poverty Truth Commission is now, in 2020, called the Poverty Truth Community. You can find out more about the community's work at: www.faithincommunity.scot/poverty-truth-community

3. www.youtube.com/watch?v=s6j_kvBdFdI

4. From *Like Leaves to the Sun: Prayers from the Iona Community*, Neil Paynter (Ed.), Wild Goose Publications, 2013

Working with people
to overcome the effects of poverty

**In the crowd**

There in the crowd.
A half-smile, world-weary but
with gestures of warmth.

There again.
Soft words, a voice of
understanding amidst pain.

A slow pace.
Walking with empathy
alongside broken hearts
and damaged lives.

Vulnerable, humble.
Unarmed.

Stuart Elliott [1]


Many members work on the ground within their communities
trying to alleviate the effects of poverty on people's lives. Unfortunately, many people now rely on food banks for sustenance.
Peter Cope, a retired Anglican minister and member living until
recently in Knighton (Powys) in Shropshire, speaks of his involvement in one that was set up in his hometown.

## The food bank, Peter Cope

Our food bank was set up by our local Churches Together group four
years ago, and I have been the chair for getting on a year now. Yes, I
know food banks are regarded with suspicion by many who see them
as blunting the need for urgent social reform in Britain, social reform
that would mean that the need for food banks would disappear

because even the poorest families would be able to afford basic food.

My reply is simply to ask: In the meantime, before this social reform goes through Parliament and gets established, how is this person going to eat who has been ill for weeks, and so suffered a reduction in wages because no sickness benefit was paid? How is this young man with mental health issues going to eat now he has been evicted from his flat? He is currently living in a tent and is not eligible for benefits because he has 'no fixed abode'. How about meals for this older woman who has got into debt and is caring for a grandchild?

We live in a little town of fewer than 4,000 people, right at the edge of mid-Wales. The nearest town accessible by bus is 30 minutes away, the nearest reasonable shopping centre almost an hour away by car. Jobs are hard to come by and several local factories have closed recently. Poverty here is certainly linked to a lack of job opportunities – but I must add that local wages are not very high. We have found that one of the most common recent reasons for seeking the help of the food bank is the introduction of Universal Credit. All claimants moved on to it must wait five weeks for their first payment; some loans are available to help people in the initial period, but these must be repaid within six months, so the cycle of debt doesn't improve very much.

The numbers of people we help are not large, as you might expect in a scattered rural community: during 2015, the busiest month was June, when we issued just over four food parcels per week, but the average throughout the year was just over two per week. For the most recent six-week period I noticed that the average is about 2.6 parcels per week – but that still means we were feeding 18 adults and one child. Each parcel has enough food for three days of meals (either for one person, or for two or three people, depending on family size); besides all the canned goods you would expect, we include toiletries, milk and dairy products, pet food as required, and often a £10 voucher to spend in our excellent local organic produce shop.

Although we have a number of enthusiastic volunteers (as you might expect), the important decision about whether to issue a food parcel is taken by our part-time manager, who is experienced, knowledgeable and compassionate. She ensures that our food bank takes referrals from social services, local health services and local clergy – and individuals can refer themselves – and we have every confidence in her. Having her on contract means that (with other necessary expenses) we have to raise about £500 per month to stay in business; fortunately, we have a number of dedicated people who support us through monthly standing orders, and we are generally well-supported by local charities.

I am very proud that the local churches and community manage to offer this support to some of the poorest in our town and area. Would we be happier if there was no need for a food bank here? Of course we would; we are not in business to enjoy ourselves playing 'Lady Bountiful' but to meet the emergency needs of the poorest in our community, and whilst those needs still exist we will be here.

*Update:* In the late autumn of 2018 we moved across the English border to Ludlow, and I became a volunteer at Ludlow Food Bank (once again sponsored by the local Churches Together), which is a much bigger operation. As I write, the coronavirus emergency and the huge disruption to employment, community and economic life it has brought is greatly adding to the number and pressure on people struggling with poverty. In the first three months of 2020, Ludlow Food Bank gave out 160 food parcels to feed 277 different individuals, an average of 21 people per week. If this rate is maintained over the rest of the year, the total for 2020 would be 640 food parcels, considerably beating the 2019 figure of 471 (itself a record year).

Other members use their work roles to enable people to receive basic support. Member Desirée van der Hijden, in the Netherlands, spoke to me about her work:

## Conversation with Desirée van der Hijden

I run a project in the hospital in Rotterdam where I work as a chaplain.

It started a few years ago because ...

You see: we work a lot with the medical social services people. There was this very senior medical social worker in the hospital trying to help a family who had lost a child, and she was so angry and so upset ...

There was literally steam coming out of her ears because she had been on the phone to the social services of the city about a child.

A child who had died just before it was born
and the parents were very poor people
(you can get extra money for extraordinary circumstances
if there is financial hardship).

She had phoned social services as she wanted them to have some money for a funeral for their child, but the woman on the phone told her:
'The family have already had extra money to buy baby stuff.
We cannot give money twice for the same child.'
My colleague hung up, and this was why she was so very upset.

So, on that occasion,
we passed around the hat, so that we could help.

But there are so many people here who are in need.

I went home and thought about it; and now we have a fund, mainly it is money from the RC diocese, not just for funerals, but to support children in the hospital.

We have to be very discreet. The hospital doesn't want people to think that, 'this is a place where you can get easy money'.

Whatever is needed,
usually it is needed quickly,
needed 'now', basically.

To get funds from social services can take up to two weeks for people who are on welfare and they will then of course have to pay it back, setting them back even further.

This makes it very difficult in an emergency situation ...

When we started, we did not have a clue what might be needed but over time we have learned that what is needed most often is ...

bus passes.

A lot of children have to stay in hospital and families want to visit. You cannot expect a young mother to get on her bike if they want to come to the hospital to see the children!

So we give them bus passes so that they can come to the hospital two or three times a day.

It has actually made a huge difference ...

some mothers already lost another child into care because they could not visit, but if they are visiting two or three times a day, they show they are willing.

That has made a difference; sometimes then they can then take the child home under supervision. It has also made a huge difference to the child who is sick.

To be visited.

Sometimes we give out money for food,
we give out money for petrol.

Two children went into intensive care and our hospital had only one bed; the other child had to go to Groningen (far away in the north).

We gave the parents money for petrol.

So the mother stayed here and the father travelled between the hospitals. And of course, they needed some money for living expenses, because the restaurant here is quite expensive.

We, as the chaplains, have discretion, so if the medical social services say, 'we do not know where to find the money', then the request comes to the chaplains and we say,

'go ahead'.
Last week it was a small computer that was needed by a child who was born with diabetes.

To monitor the child's blood sugar the family needed a computer. So that the child wouldn't have to come to hospital each day. And, of course, the family did not have one.

In Rotterdam, there are many very poor people. So, whatever we feel is needed, we help with.

We give, we don't let people know where the money comes from.

People don't need to know that; they don't need to feel grateful.

They don't know it is church money.

If they ask, we tell them, but on the whole, they don't ask. They are just very happy that they get help. And it is just simple, practical things, without making them jump through hoops.

For example, sometimes someone may need a breast pump to take milk to a baby. Or it could be something simple like a cake, if the person has a birthday while in hospital.

It's not going to make a big difference, but it is something.

People feel appreciated.

Most of the people have major problems. A bus pass or a cake isn't going to put their life straight. But we notice that they grow stronger and more resourceful through being given just a little trust, a little help.

It has also made a big difference to the staff, those who work with social services,
those who were getting so unhappy and frustrated ...

Because, they see the need is real, and they want to help. They are now able to say to the families:

'I might be able to find a little money to help you.'

It does not cost that much; basically,
we only spend about 1000-1500 euros a year.

We also tap into the parish churches of Rotterdam for help. There are many poor people in that area, so they know where to find cheap clothes, cradles, chairs, whatever.

I always have a bag of baby clothes in my room, just for emergencies ...

People like being able to do something; even people from the parish where I live, which is south of Rotterdam, have started giving me things so that I can pass them on.

*Sue:*

Why do you see it as important to do this?

*Desirée:*

It is about social justice.
It is also about seeing …

It is looking at people and really seeing what they may need, and I have found that a lot of Christian people are very willing to help other people but they are not seeing the need, or asking the right questions …

especially when it comes to money.

They develop a blindness, an embarrassment. You don't usually ask, 'Do you have money to do this?'
'Can you afford it?'
'Are you in work?'

It's the same when I worked in a parish …
People's needs can be seen, if you have eyes that see, and ears that listen.

With the Iona Community, we work through ordinary things and ordinary life. For example, a child is lacking a bicycle to go to school. If we see and hear this, the Kingdom of God comes nearer to us.

It is about seeing things as they are and poor people not being seen as an embarrassment or a 'them', as in: 'Let's help them.' But we need to see this is a concrete need, and that they have a right to live their life as much as I do.

This thing about funerals.

I think it is completely terrible that in the city of Rotterdam you would not pay, in these kind of circumstances, for the funeral of a child.

As if people are out to get a free funeral!

No one wants there to be a funeral, because they don't want their children to die. They don't expect them to die. They are people just like me. Not some underclass.

Poor people are often looked at as an underclass.

*Sue:*

In the UK – I cannot speak for the Netherlands – there seems to be prejudice and disparity between the people who are on benefits and those who are not.

*Desirée:*

Basically, they could be you and me, and given chances, they will be like you and me. Most of them were very able to lead their lives before …

this particular event happened,
this disaster struck.

There often is a precarious balance. They don't expect me to shell out thousands of euros, but just enough for bus passes or just to get them through the time at the hospital.

Bus passes are not going to save lives. But it's important they are there when you really, really need them. When you need to be with your son or daughter. Then you can work out the rest of your life yourself.

The difference between a child being alone in hospital and a parent being with them is huge.

It is life-changing for both of them.

It also helps them show people …
'Look: I am a young mum; I don't have much,
but I can care for my child.'

Fortunately, we don't have too many young mums these days but there are still women who have three or four children with different fathers, and often the new fathers don't like the other children.

But being there for the child can give a bond between mother and child that changes their lives.

It is a very small thing really.

*Sue:*

I think it is all the small grains of sand that make up the north end beach on Iona!

*Desirée:*

That is true!

Sometimes being involved with projects set up to alleviate the effects of poverty in a different part of the UK or the world can enable you to think about how you can support your own community in better ways. Norman Shanks, a former Leader of the Iona Community, talked to me about a project he and his wife, Ruth, volunteered with while he was on sabbatical in the U.S.

## Open Door Community, Norman Shanks

I spent one month as a resident volunteer at the Open Door Community (or 910, as it was known) in Atlanta in 2001. For over 30 years until the closure of its Atlanta building, and now continuing since its move to Baltimore, it has exercised an impressive and hospitable ministry among homeless people and campaigned faithfully against racism, poverty and the death penalty. Even more effectively than the Iona Community, I believe, the Open Door embodies an integrated approach to spirituality – holding together work and worship, prayer and politics, treating the people it serves with great sensitivity and compassion. Two of the Open Door founders/leaders came to lead a week on Iona in 2002; and Ruth and I spent much time at the Open Door when we were in Atlanta for three months in the autumn of 2007, when I was visiting scholar at Columbia Theological Seminary, Decatur.

Ruth also told me about her time volunteering at Open Door, helping with breakfast on Tuesdays, assisting at the foot clinic on Thursday evenings and sharing in the Communion and meal on Sundays. She realised that she could offer foot clinics to homeless people when she returned home to Glasgow. Ruth wrote of her experiences in *Coracle*, the magazine of the Iona Community:

## The foot clinic, Ruth Douglas Shanks

Open Door was a powerful, heart-warming and memorable experience for me, out of which grew the idea of starting a foot clinic in Glasgow. I realised I could use my skills as a physiotherapist in the sort of way I had been looking for since retiring. So I approached the Lodging House Mission, a church-related day centre in Glasgow's East End mostly for folk who are homeless or in hostels and supported accommodation, about the possibility of starting a foot clinic there, and they readily agreed. The plan was to base the practicalities broadly on what would happen each week at the Open Door, although I recognised that there would be significant differences due to the context and culture (and I've certainly discovered that most of the people who come to the foot clinic are better-off than those we dealt with in Atlanta, owing to the lack of welfare benefits in the U.S.). Some of the local churches helped with donations of footbaths, sprays, scrubs, creams, towels, scissors, clippers and so on, as well as giving money, and this generosity is ongoing. Initially Alison Macdonald (then an associate member of the Community, since sadly died) helped me, then Community

Members Duncan Finlayson, Caro Penney and Katy Owen. Several years on, until Covid-19 caused the lockdown, Katy and I have been going fortnightly and the foot clinic has continued to thrive.

What happens each fortnight on Tuesday mornings? We rely on people referring themselves, so introductions, initial conversations and explanations of what we do are important. People can naturally be apprehensive; taking off your socks and shoes for this purpose makes you vulnerable (and you can't escape in a hurry!), people can be embarrassed about dirty feet and so on. Clearly, we are not trained podiatrists. What we offer is foot washing, using foot-spas, basic chiropody (e.g. cutting nails, removing hard skin and corns), massage and general advice on footwear, foot care and other minor problems (e.g. muscle strains, infections). We have a supply of shoes and socks. As well as giving advice, if there are more serious problems we encourage the men and women to attend a nearby medical clinic. The maximum number of people we have treated in the two-hour period is 12, and it tends to vary each time, depending on how long it takes to deal with each person who comes.

We deliberately sit at a lower level than the folk who come. Apart from being more comfortable and the practical reasons relating to foot treatment, it puts the relationship on a more level playing field, and we feel this is important. After all, in what's happening the vulnerability is mutual – for the giver as well as the receiver – and this helps achieve a sense of sharing and equality in this basic and intimate task.

Why is this important to us and how does it relate to our faith? In general, the folk who come initiate, and we are keen to engage in conversation about their story and circumstances; and we often have the sense of opportunities missed and young lives wasted. Occasionally they ask us why we are doing this. Sometimes they tell us about their family and how they became homeless – very often because of family break-up and addiction problems. They often speak of their dream to be in some sort of employment (even more difficult, of course, in the present economic situation) and mention people who have helped them at some point along the way; such names (familiar within the Community) as Colin Anderson, John Miller and Betty White have cropped up!

As far as the faith dimension goes, I feel there is something sacramental in what we are doing. Jesus cared for the marginalised and needy, washed the feet of the disciples and told his followers to do likewise in loving and caring for one another. One example of this is Mary, who according to the Gospels washed the feet of Jesus using expensive ointment, even before he washed the disciples' feet; so Mary can be seen as the model disciple. And I'm reminded too of the old saying, which happens to be prominently displayed just inside the entrance of the Open Door: *'Often we meet Christ in the stranger's guise.'* [2]

Ruth e-mailed me recently and told me more:

Now, eight or so years on, as well as continuing with this work, Katy Owen and I have also started a foot clinic at a night shelter, run by the Glasgow Destitution Network in Anderston Kelvingrove Church, where for an evening every three weeks or so we have met asylum-seekers (who are seeking 'the right to remain') from many countries across the world. This is an entirely different experience from what I described in the *Coracle* article: for example, it is a much more fluctuating population that we see, with people coming and going week by week; and many are traumatised and desperate; some have just arrived, often after a horrific journey, and some have been 'waiting' here for several years. They enjoy the sense of community at the night shelter, which they see as home, and seem to be very grateful for the support and time we spend with them – just as we appreciate, very much, the opportunity we have to help them.

(*Note:* Subsequently the night shelter had to move from Anderston Kelvingrove to temporary accommodation, where space was limited and it was not possible for the foot clinic to continue. Now planning is progressing towards a move to a permanent home.)

## Prayer

*We stand together you and I.*
*I reach out my hand to you,*
*you reach out your hand to take mine,*
*and we walk together*
*on a journey of discovery*
*that will leave both of us changed,*
*transformed.*

Susan Dale

## Sources and notes

1. Written for Pax Christi Sunday. From Stuart Elliott's website: www.reluctantordinand.co.uk

2. From *Coracle*, the magazine of the Iona Community, 2011, Neil Paynter (Ed.)

Working for mental and spiritual wellbeing

The lily tilts its head to the moonlight,
ethereal beams of light
shine down.
It is washed now by the grace
of planets unknown;
connected through an umbilical of hope.

That same light is a light from the heavens.
From the light come the angels,
angels so beautiful beyond humanity's eye.
Their gaze caresses my soul.
They link my insubstantial life
to that of the divine.
They forgive my weakness
and take away my fear
giving hope of a life beyond what is now.

Aabira

## Aabira's story

The doctors at the hospital tied a label onto me – 'depression' – but it is not a language I understand. It comes from a different dimension where Allah, may His name be praised, does not exist, and family and cultural boundaries mean nothing. I cannot live with that label any more. All things have a meaning and will be resolved.

Writing my story and having it honoured and respected by others means much; and having it told, in ways that empower me, strengthens my resolve. As I write, I understand more of what has been my life, and what is important. My life has grown into meaning, into more than any earthly pain endured. It is through my prayer and thought that I am enriched. My past has pain in it, but even this has given something to my life. Without it I would not be reliant on a life of prayer, and it is through this prayer that I am transformed.

I cannot change what has happened, but I can embrace the teachings of Mohammed, may His name be praised, and this depression flees. I change my name to Aabira; a strong woman who knows Islam.

Having the freedom to write and rewrite, and talk with someone, even though she came from a different faith, has helped me. Always having to live within mental health definitions is like living within the walls of a prison. I ask you, 'Is it therapeutic to shut out the divine?' [1]

Many Iona Community members, including myself, work in roles that encompass psychotherapy, counselling, pastoral care and spiritual accompaniment, with people of all faiths, and none. One thing I have discovered over the years is that being a therapist means listening, but it is also about learning from those you listen to. This learning can take many forms; sometimes it leads to exploration and growth. Aabira is an inspirational young woman and her own exploration of what spirituality means to her as a Muslim enabled me, a middle-aged Christian, to glimpse something of what the relationship with the divine means to me. Some years later Aabira travelled to Iona and stayed as a guest at the MacLeod Centre. She e-mailed me, telling me about her experience:

A place of extraordinary courage. With its beautiful sea and sand, it stands testament to people's willingness to embrace the other and grapple with what it means to be a community. I, as a Muslim, felt welcomed and enabled by the experience.

My mental health has been fragile over the years. Strangely, it is within the betwixt and between of different faiths that I have found a healing space.

Aabira's question, 'Is it therapeutic to shut out the divine?' resonates deeply with me, and brings a somewhat opposite yet linked question to mind: 'Is it right within our Christian ministry to shut out mental health concerns?'

I talked about this with Stephen Wright, a member from Cumbria. Stephen is the Resident Spiritual Director of the Sacred Space Foundation, a charity which *'for nearly 30 years, has provided safe space for rest and reflection with one-to-one, personalised support from experienced and compassionate spiritual directors and guides'*. The charity seeks to support spiritual seekers from different religions, and none, without judgement or dogma (www.sacredspace.org.uk).

Stephen told me that there are lots of places in Cumbria that are 'outward bound' and focus on engaging with the environment and physical health. He sees the work at Sacred Space as being more about the journey 'inward bound'.

## Sacred Space, Stephen Wright

Within the Rule of the Iona Community, I've had to pledge myself to action for peace and justice, and I have sometimes felt that if I am not chaining myself to the barricades, or lining up in some demo, then perhaps I am not quite cutting the mustard. Perhaps that is partly because so much of the work that I do, and that Sacred Space provides, is 'invisible'. Many of the people who come to us are in crisis, disconnected from the Source, internally and externally, and are often dealing with some sort of strife in life, such as facing an injustice problem at work, at home or with the law.

I think of the individuals we meet, in their search for inner peace and perhaps outer peace with some setting with which they are in conflict.

Then there is also the group work: a quiet presence in organisations, where there is a need for conflict resolution, when relationships in teams or between organisations and employees have broken down; also, the running of retreats using our local diocesan facilities for NHS staff.

I think also of the compassion work we do with teams of (mainly) health care staff that is important too ... predicated on helping to make others feel whole, who then go out into the world to do what they do from a much more integrated place in themselves.

That leads me on to reflect on the way each of us goes about 'living' our Rule, like me in more invisible ways, in the way I participate in church, village and family life. I've been struck by some Iona Community members I've met who are out there putting the world to rights, but who have dysfunctional families and workplaces or who are angry and burned out ... i.e., not walking our talk.

John Polhill is another member who, with his wife, Christine, works within that threshold that lies somewhere between spirituality and mental wellbeing. He wrote to me about the Hermitage/Reflection Gardens, which he and Christine founded near Lichfield.

## The Hermitage/Reflection Gardens, John Polhill

Around 25 years ago, when our sons were in their late teens, we had a kind of fantasy game in which someone came up with an idea and we all expanded it into a highly improbable conclusion. And so it was that on a walk in the Chilterns on New Year's Day, that we took up my wife Christine's suggestion that she would like to plant some trees in memory of her uncle, and developed it into a large-scale environmental project. It involved buying a derelict farm, planting a large woodland and using the outbuildings to house arts and crafts activities.

We had had a very difficult and stressful family year and this walk marked a turning point, as the Holy Spirit seemed to be part of the conversation and the idea stayed.

When we got back home I wrote down all the different things we could do, and we started by trying to persuade the St Albans diocese to be part of the project through glebe land. This did not work out, so we wrote to all the dioceses that had a community forest within their boundaries, and began a conversation with the Lichfield diocese. When I was able to take early retirement, I enrolled on two courses in arboriculture and began to look for a site. We had been inspired by the embryonic environmental movement, the Iona pilgrimage, the need to make connections between Christianity and care for nature, the Ignatian spiritual exercises, and the extraordinary things that members of the Community were doing.

And then, as I started to examine possible locations, reality began to rear its ugly head. Just when all seemed lost, however, I was led by a series of events to an old bungalow with a large garden on the edge of a forest designated as an Area of Outstanding Natural Beauty, situated 20 miles north of Birmingham. I often ask myself how and why I became so confident that this was the place – an area of the country we didn't know, a property we wouldn't previously have dreamt of buying, a setting far short of the dream and, indeed, Christine and I with no clear plan about what it might become. My conclusion is that if you have a strong vision, it will carry you to a place in which a dream can become an appropriate reality.

So, starting in 1998, we had the bungalow rebuilt and extended, hired a garden designer and a man with a JCB, found a local mental health project that did gardening work, and slogged away for around five years laying paths and fences, digging and planting, managing weeds and building water features. Then, we watched it all mature. The garden design is of five separate areas with five-foot hedges, each themed on the Spiritual Exercises of St Ignatius of Loyola together with an environmental issue. The designer suggested a pathway through the gardens that forms a complete circuit, just like the Iona pilgrimage. People came to see it right from the beginning, when some of the 'garden' was still mud and undeveloped.

Then two really helpful things happened: I used my New members project to build a website (with help from my son); and we got planning permission to convert one of the (two!) double garages into a self-catering unit ('the Hermitage') that could also be used as a meeting space. Our individual visitors, who mostly find us through the website, come for a day or stay for up to a week (or two months in one case!) and groups come to visit the gardens or just use the meeting room. Some visitors ask to see Christine for spiritual direction/companionship, and some groups ask us to lead a quiet day or participate in their programme. We don't make a fixed charge, but invite visitors to make a donation to the charity we set up to fund the project.

Were it not for Christine's idea of putting a visitors' book in the Hermitage, we wouldn't have known much about visitors' experience of the gardens and the accommodation. Some people might describe the entries as 'humbling', but I have found them so encouraging. I have ceased to regard the gardens and the Hermitage as things that we created, but as entities in themselves for which we are stewards. I often tell visitors that I had intended to create 'unquiet gardens', especially in respect of the environmental content. What I have discovered is that people find these issues so threatening, and that it is only because they find the gardens so peaceful that they are able to engage with the content.

And so, this is how we live out the main part of our peace and justice commitment, along with various environmental projects and running a mental health charity. It seems, sometimes, rather too enjoyable compared with the things others do, but I guess that actually most people enjoy this part of the Rule, however they choose to practise it.

As we have heard, members such as Stephen, John and Christine sometimes spend years creating places like the Sacred Space Foundation and the Hermitage and Reflection Gardens, places people can visit or be part of. At other times, members react to circumstances that unfold around them in their own communities. When a five-year-old child named April Jones was murdered in Machynlleth, the small town in Wales where I lived, the local community and the Iona Community started a project to support local people through what was an extremely stressful time. The project was set up (including finding the funding) within six weeks of the murder. I wrote in my journal at the time:

*November 2012*

*There is just so much grief. There are police searchers everywhere, looking, I fear, for a small body.*

*We have lost a child; she has been murdered by a member of our own community. How will we as a community support each other? Messages of support start to come in for the community from around the world, and in my own personal e-mail account, messages of support, prayer and love from fellow Iona Community members. Resilience sometimes is not so much about stamina or personal strength, but about being part of a community, who do not all think the same but who draw together around you at a time of crisis, offering encouragement, nurture and just walking alongside.*

The project in Machynlleth ran for two years, staffed by a dedicated team of volunteer listeners and counsellors, and offered a confidential counselling service, a drop-in for informal support and a telephone helpline. Together we stood alongside the community through the UK's largest ever police search operation, the trial and the funeral. I have written much elsewhere about the project in Machynlleth. (See *Threads of Hope: Counselling and Emotional Support Services for Communities in Crisis*, Cambridge Scholars Publishing, 2016.) The Iona

Community provided support on so many levels, through prayer, funding and being there with us every step of the way. Anna Briggs, a Community member who at the time lived in Thurso, sent a parcel of shawls, which brought comfort to April's family and friends. Ruth Burgess, a member living in Dunblane, sent a prayer just at the right moment, at a time of intolerable waiting for news. The prayer appeared on noticeboards and in churches all over the town:

**We wait, Ruth Burgess**

In quiet and in sadness,
we wait.
With questions and anger,
we wait.
With friends and with family,
we wait.
We wait and we cry, 'How long?'

In the morning and the evening,
we wait.
As the world goes on around us,
we wait.
With an emptiness inside us,
we wait.
We wait and we cry, 'How long?'

With the town of Machynlleth,
we wait.
With our children and our neighbours,
we wait.
With all who are sad and exhausted,
we wait.
We wait and we cry, 'How long?' [2]

Ruth Burgess

## Sources and notes

1. 'Aabira's story' is published in full in *Thresholds*, the British Association for Counselling and Psychotherapy's quarterly journal, autumn, 2012

2. From *Saying Goodbye: Resources for Funerals, Scattering Ashes and Remembering*, Wild Goose Publications, Ruth Burgess (Ed.), 2013

Hospitality: Welcoming refugees and asylum-seekers

Hospitality in its truest form is offering space to another person unconditionally.

Member Sally Beaumont wrote to me from Glasgow, where over the last 10 years she has hosted about 25 asylum-seekers. Here are just a few of the stories she tells.

## Asylum-seekers' stories, Sally Beaumont

I have always tried to remember that the people I welcome into my home are just normal people who need to sleep and eat. I try to keep a normal structure, not stepping out of my own routine and not going overboard. I am sharing a home, and this adds colour to my life.

Some of the folk who have stayed here are now my friends, with whom I share stories and memories. Perhaps we did not laugh at the time, but now, looking back, we can laugh.

Some of the food I cooked was strange to them and they did not like it, but often felt they could not say so. If I asked a question, often they gave me the answer that they thought I wanted to hear, rather than what they really thought! Sometimes they cooked food for me, usually either very spicy, or the opposite, very bland. They all certainly added spice to my day.

### Zahir from Afghanistan

Zahir spoke good English. His language was colourful, staccato and often abbreviated. His first language was Pashto. I never fully discovered his background. He told me after a few days that his father had been a general and he had been a soldier. His father had been killed in an ambush and at that same time Zahir had lost his eye. He had had to flee. How he had arrived in Glasgow I do not know, but he was obviously vulnerable and needed asylum. He was a very tall man with a good physique; the loss of his eye made his face lopsided and gave him a threatening expression.

The first morning I asked him if he had slept well. Hesitation. Should he be polite, or tell it as it was?

'No,' he said, 'the cover is too short.' He explained, miming, that if he put the duvet over his head, like at home, his feet stuck out; if it covered his feet, his head was cold! I found another blanket and also suggested a hot-water bottle. With a slightly pained expression, he said, 'I don't drink hot water.' I showed him the hot-water bottle and his expression turned into a smile. Every morning he brought it through to the kitchen, remarking what a wonderful thing it was. It intrigued him so much I gave it to him when he left.

He was always interested in talking and told me a little of his childhood. This made him very sorrowful. He loved television and would still be watching at 2 or 3am. I came in late one night and he was watching some important snooker match. He asked me if I knew the game. I did not answer as I wanted to go to bed, but a fulsome, detailed explanation followed. He had had a snooker table at home, so I heard a little more of his background.

He would use the Internet on my computer and obviously understood the intricacies of it. Asylum-seekers very often have such skills and abilities, and in most cases they want to work – in fact, above all else they desire to work. It seems ironic that the government does not allow them to work and thus provide for themselves and pay taxes.

Zahir received his Section 4, which allows for the provision of support for failed asylum-seekers, and disappeared from my life.

## Mary from Zimbabwe

Mary was in her 20s and was a member of a Pentecostal church. She came to me from Positive Action in Housing (www.paih.org). She arrived alone and unaccompanied; because her English was very good, PAIH thought giving her instructions to my flat was adequate. They told her to take a number 44 bus and ask the driver to let her off at the Hyndland shops. He forgot, and she rode on to the terminus. The bus driver apologised. Fortunately, Mary had been given my phone number so she was able to call me; I could tell from her voice that she had a bad cold. I explained that she needed to cross over the road and take the bus back; fortunately, PAIH had provided her with enough money to cover the next fare, as she herself had no funds. I suggested that she ask loudly at each stop whether this was the Hyndland shops. I thought someone would eventually get fed up and tell her they knew the shops and would let her know where to get off, and this, indeed, was what happened. Meanwhile, at home, I was in a quandary: a long time had elapsed and I needed to go out. I phoned my daughter, Jackie, who agreed to come and hold the fort. As Jackie was driving to my house, she spied an African woman carrying her luggage along the street, and asked her if she was going to Sally's. 'Yes, my name is Mary,' she said. By the time I got home she was tucked up in bed with a Lemsip.

Next morning, I met her for the first time. She was a bonny girl with an attractive smile and a delightful laugh, who, I was soon to learn, was fairly streetwise. Life had dealt her many blows, though, so these facial expressions were not always present. She had had to leave Zimbabwe because of the deteriorating political situation. She had met other asylum-seekers like herself at PAIH; and, once her cold had improved, she set out one morning to meet with one of these Zimbabwean friends, saying she would be back that evening for a meal.

The evening meal passed; 10pm came and went; and 11pm; then midnight. At 1am I went to bed, leaving Mary's bedroom door open (she had keys). At 4am, I woke and went to check her door and it was shut.

I knocked on her door at 10am and heard her jump out of bed and fling the door open.

'It's a miracle! It's a miracle!' she shouted.

Somewhat astounded, I awaited an explanation. The story emerged slowly. She had overlooked telling me that her friend was 37 weeks pregnant. They had been window-shopping in Sauchiehall Street when, without warning, her friend's waters broke and labour started. Mary knew she could call 999 without credit, so she did. Soon an ambulance arrived, and they were taken to the Royal Infirmary. Her friend begged her to stay with her as she had nobody to call, the baby's father having disappeared several months previously. Later that night, as her friend held Mary's hand, a baby girl was born. This was the miracle – the birth of a baby.

Later the following day, Mary visited the hospital, where mother and baby were being discharged back to a small flat in Govan. Mary went with them on the bus, the baby wrapped in a towel. Each day Mary visited and was as helpful as she could be.

As with the others, Mary's Section 4 eventually came through and she was given accommodation.

### Michael from Zimbabwe

A word or two here about Zimbabwe. This is a country, once known as 'the bread basket of Africa', which has been devastated in recent years. Any sign of complaint can and will be met with arrest, imprisonment or, worse, disappearance. I have received many people from Zimbabwe. This is not the only country to which the UK does not return people; the same is true of Iraq, Afghanistan, Somalia and Eritrea. It is not always the case that people from these countries can stay, however; they have to provide evidence of danger and persecution, which is often extremely difficult to obtain, given that they have had to flee for their lives.

Michael arrived one evening, tired and dispirited. After something to eat, he said he wished to go to bed. Before he went, he asked me if I had any Christian books. This was an excellent question to ask in my house. I found him four books very quickly. Next morning he got up late, remarking that despite his tiredness one of the books had captured his imagination and he had read until the early hours.

Later that morning I was invited to a friend's house for coffee, so asked Michael if he would like to come along. One of the problems these guests of mine have is that they are not allowed to work, they usually do not know their way around and, even if they do, they have no money for buses or little treats like coffee, so time often hangs heavily on their hands. Michael and I set off in the rain, and it was not until we were halfway there that I realised we were going to have coffee with the author of the book he had been reading so avidly! I stopped and told him; he too stopped and said, 'What! What! I do not believe it – we are actually going to have coffee with the author of that wonderful book. Can I ask her questions?' I suggested he did just that. Kathy (Galloway) was happy to answer his questions, and I learned a good bit too.

Michael also came to church with me, and discovered there was a drumming group there that met weekly. He was a drummer and enjoyed attending their meetings while he was with me. This did not last long as fairly soon he was given accommodation.

He was having problems picking up his vouchers each week, and on one occasion I accompanied him. At that time they were being given out by a private company. Seeing the attitude of the company and the difficulties it put in the way of claimants was an eye-opener for me.

*Sylla from Guinea*

My phone rang one cold snowy day in 2010; it was PAIH, asking me to take in Sylla. They told me she only spoke French. I do not speak French. They mentioned that she was distressed and needed some 'tender, loving care'. I suggested they ask a host who spoke French.

Two hours later they phoned again to say they had had no luck, so I said yes. Sylla, a downcast woman in her 30s, duly arrived, tired and tear-stained. She drank a cup of tea and indicated by miming that she wanted to sleep. I gave her keys to the flat and assured her that I would be in if she needed anything. As with Zahir from Afghanistan, I gave her a fleece-covered hot-water bottle, which I hoped would comfort her. She took it to bed.

Next morning she appeared looking neither rested nor well, carrying a brown envelope and a brown-paper parcel. These she handed to me, so I realised I was meant to open them. The envelope contained several copies of a letter from a consultant at Gartnavel Hospital, addressed to the Home Office. I read the letter with a sinking heart. It started, 'Should the recipient of this letter intend to return this woman to her country of origin they will be signing her death warrant.' It then detailed all her medical problems, of which I understood only one: she had HIV/AIDS. The parcel contained her antiretroviral drugs and other medication, which were to be kept in the fridge. I deposited them there and helped her with the instructions, mainly by miming. I did have some long-forgotten French but it was not like her French, obviously. In fact, the next few days improved both our miming skills.

Sylla slept a great deal and slowly her appetite increased. She watched television and spent time in her room. I did invite a friend to coffee who spoke fluent French. This certainly improved understanding, but apparently Sylla's Guinea French and my friend's French were not exactly compatible.

After two or three days, Sylla's mobile phone rang; she answered and, getting very agitated, handed the phone to me. A man's voice spoke in English and told me that he had met Sylla at the PAIH offices, where they had both had to wait for many hours. He said that Sylla had been very distressed and he had tried to comfort her. The caller was from Zimbabwe, an asylum-seeker like her. He was living in Hamilton and had promised to phone her to see how she was. He said he would like to meet her and take her out for coffee. She understood this and suggested the bus station – she kept repeating, 'bus station, bus station'. So it was agreed that he would be at the information desk at the bus station at one o'clock. After my attempted explanations and mimes of how to get to the bus station, Sylla set off in the snow.

Hours later, my phone rang. It was him again, asking whether she had returned. He explained that he had phoned her mobile at one o'clock, and she said she was in the bus station but could not describe where. He had hunted for her for an hour but never found her. I think she had never actually been at the right place.

It was still snowing. A miserable, dejected figure appeared an hour later and went to bed. I felt so sorry, but helpless.

After a week, PAIH sent a caseworker for Sylla as they had found somewhere for her to stay. This was not before she had graphically mimed to me how four soldiers had abducted her husband at gunpoint and each had then raped her. I can only assume that this is why she had AIDS. I suppose there are many like her. My horror must have shown and she broke down in tears.

Words failed me. What comfort could I give her? As she left, I gave her the hot-water bottle, and she smiled.

I often think of Sylla and wonder how and where she is now. This was a difficult time, but even so there were laughs with Sylla as both of us tried to mime things.

How Sylla had come to the UK and to Glasgow I do not know. She had been evicted from her first accommodation in Glasgow and been referred to the Scottish Refugee Council, who had sent her to PAIH.

## Sha-Ling from China

If you leave China with no appropriate travel documents China will not allow you back into the country. Somehow or another, Sha-Ling had arrived here. She stayed with several hosts and came to me for only a few days when one of the other hosts was away. Her English was very basic, but the most important factor for her was that she was nearly seven months pregnant. This meant she could not be deported and would be supported. She had some money from PAIH and was anxious to cook her own food, which she had bought herself. She was extremely polite and always tidied up after her cooking, often tidying up after mine too. She was small and neat, despite her pregnancy, and anxious to learn.

One incident I remember well, because it was one of those problem-solving conundrums. I have no way of knowing how accurate this supposition was but I had guessed that Sha-Ling had been persecuted for being a Christian, and so her parents had organised a way of spiriting her out of the country. I asked her if she went to church and her response was a shake of the head. I asked her whether she was a Christian – a shake of the head. I asked her if she had a Bible – a shake of the head. A few hours later she appeared in the kitchen wearing a tiny silver crucifix. I smiled and gently approached her and put my hand under the cross, remarking how lovely it was. She smiled. I then got paper and pencil. In an unconvincing manner, I drew a church; I drew a cross. I disappeared to return with my Bible. Her reaction was a broad grin. She disappeared and returned with a book, which looked written in Chinese, and which I took to be a Bible. She studied my book and I hers. Then an idea crossed my mind.

We looked at the contents pages displaying the names and pages of all the books. They appeared to be the same. Next, we numbered all the books in pencil, with '1' meaning the Old Testament and '2' meaning the New Testament – and so we were both ready to go to church cradling our respective Bibles. She was able to find the Chinese equivalent as I scribbled down the numbers when they were read out, and could read along with us.

Sha-Ling was not well and often in pain while she stayed with me, spending most of her time indoors. Then she moved on.

However, I did keep up with her – and she had a beautiful baby boy. My daughter and I helped with clothes, pram and baby goods. She has been accommodated in a pleasant house, which she shares with another asylum-seeker. Being a young mother alone with a new baby in a strange country, not knowing the language, is very hard to imagine. I know I would not have liked to be in her shoes.

*Karim from Iraq*

A tentative voice, which I recognised as being from PAIH, sounded on the phone. Would it be possible for me to take someone in that day? I answered yes, and waited for more. 'Well ... you see ... we have to find him a place ... as the hospital wish to discharge him.' Aha! Here came the explanation.

Karim was a 23-year-old Iraqi who had been set upon and had his face slashed in a Glasgow street. The hospital had stitched him up and realigned his jaw. His wounds were healing and he did not require any more medical attention. However, he needed a safe place with a caring person to accommodate him. PAIH did not want to place him in a hostel, understandably.

As soon as he arrived, accompanied by a worker from PAIH, I beheld a bloody, bandaged head, slashes down through the forehead, cheek and chin covered with Micropore tape; all of this above a well-muscled, fit, sturdy, hard body. What was this? I wondered. We did not talk much but I could tell from the little we did that his English, though not perfect, was good. He looked very dejected and tired, so immediately after something to eat he retired to bed.

Next day, he kept to his room and I was out much of the time. The following day he had his stitches taken out at the hospital, and returned to my flat looking very much improved. That evening he was talkative. He came to the kitchen and handed me a brown envelope. Imagine my surprise when I found myself staring at a big photo of Karim wearing full military gear, firearms and all, beside a man I recognised from the TV. The President of Iraq. Karim had been one of his bodyguards, hence the strapping physique. He explained that in Iraq he had received several death threats as a result of his work. The perpetrators accused him of being in the pay of the Americans. The President insisted on him leaving Iraq and provided him with passport, papers, visa and money to come to the UK. He made his way to Glasgow for the simple reason that he had some Iraqi friends here. This had all happened six or eight months previously. By now, his money had run out, his visa was out of date and he was dependent on his friends. The incident in Sauchiehall Street had brought the police and the ambulance service to the scene. When his identity was discovered, it resulted in him having to claim asylum. Now he was on the police radar.

The next part of the story was interesting. While here in Glasgow, he met and fell for a Scottish woman with whom he spent much time. They were walking along together, in broad daylight, when to his astonishment another man with a knife jumped him from a doorway, slashing his face and knocking him about before taking to his heels. Later it became clearer; seemingly, the attacker was Karim's girlfriend's ex-boyfriend, whom she had ditched. He had been stalking her, phoning her day and night, following her about and not taking no for an answer. He was now being sought by the police.

After 10 days or so, Karim received his accommodation and Azure card under section 4, which meant he had to leave my flat: he had received his marching orders. (The Home Office always needs to know people's whereabouts.)

This was not before another incident occurred. Karim would use my computer each day, usually to look up Al Jazeera and other Arabic programmes. I was out one morning, having already opened my computer. When I got home later, I couldn't power it up. I tried various switches and fiddled with it without success. Then I heard Karim come in. His first words were, 'I did wrong.' He had accidentally stepped on the multi-plug and damaged the switch. At once he had phoned his girlfriend and they had been out to buy a new one. It emerged from a plastic bag, was fitted and all was well.

When Karim left he thanked me graciously, but his suggestion of keeping in touch with me by coming to the church where he had once accompanied me has never materialised.

Penny and Geoff Gardner, who live in Dorset, became associate members of the Community about 10 years ago, having come to Christianity 20 years previously, in their 40s.

## Sherborne Area Refugee Support, Penny Gardner

I visited Iona with some friends who had been there many times, and found out about this group of people from all over the world who did not seem to be afraid to share their faith at a very honest and basic level. I was excited about the discussions I was part of during the week, and later did my best to convey this to my husband, Geoff.

Finally, Geoff and I were able to visit Iona together. It was a week full of sunshine – as opposed to the torrential summer rain of my first visit! The discussions we had, the people we met, the songs we sang and the worship moved us a great deal. We began to question our involvement within our own community – as well as within the Iona Community.

During the first evening service on Iona we were lucky enough to break and share cookies with Rosemary and Stephen Rymer, who were from our part of the country. Though it was some months before we were to see them again, it was a significant meeting.

We met the Rymers again at a gathering of Iona associates in the area. At the time, they were contemplating becoming members of the Community and were already part of an Iona Family Group. We were searching for an extension/expression of our faith. We had moved to a new town, Sherborne, and thought this might be the opportunity to worship differently. We, too, became part of the Family Group.

Like a door opening, we found ourselves attending monthly meetings and listening to stories from people who had been Christians far longer than ourselves. They seemed to know so much about the Bible, and every time we met we came away feeling grateful for the opportunity to share our faith and hear about others' ways of expressing theirs. We were in awe of their involvement within their own communities – with peace and justice, education, politics, environmental concerns ... We toyed with ways of becoming involved ourselves.

I mentioned to them my reluctance to stick my head above the parapet. (I am American and could easily be shown the door out of the UK.) I remember being encouraged to just 'go for it'.

Not long after this, Geoff and I began to feel desperate about the plight of refugees in Europe.

At about this time I found out that my previously prosperous brother, who lived in the U.S., had lost everything and was sick and unable to pay for medical attention. Soon he was living on the streets. Despite our efforts, he was killed in a traffic accident whilst homeless.

The homelessness; the families left with nothing. The sadness crept in and initially overwhelmed us. But while attending a meeting of Churches Together in our town, I mentioned our concern about the refugees. The chairman felt immediately that Churches Together should lead the way, and called a meeting of anyone who would be interested in doing something.

A group of about 50 people met to exchange information and ideas. Most of the group were older people, but Mia, a young woman (23 years old), suddenly spoke up. She had been working with refugees in Birmingham when she was at university, and she began to give us some facts about the needs of those coming to the UK.

After the meeting I rang Mia and we met. Her complete immersion in the cause of refugees was apparent. She was the rep for Refugees Welcome UK (www.refugees-welcome.net); and soon we were planning a larger meeting with a guest speaker from Refugees Welcome.

It was an exciting meeting, with people from neighbouring towns and even some from further away. The speaker from Refugees Welcome was incredible – and by the end of the meeting everyone left with a job to do.

It was a busy month. Estate agents were approached for housing, and Mia and her committee met with the local MP to ask for his support. They didn't get any. Dorset was staying put and not accepting any refugees. Some of us approached schools, and others thought of ways to raise awareness. Refugees Welcome UK taught us how to exchange ideas with others instead of just talking on and on about the problem of refugees.

A month passed, and it seemed as though we'd made no progress. We sat with Mia over coffee and cake and talked about what we could do. Mia is never without her phone and she relayed the latest news from the refugee camp in Calais. We half-heartedly mulled over the idea of going over there as volunteers. The Christmas break was approaching and we realised, suddenly, that we had the time. Before the end of the day, we had decided to go to Calais the following week. There were several people who wanted to go with us, including my granddaughter, who was then 16. The others were in their teens or 20s. Geoff and I are in our 70s; it took no time at all, however, for us to commit to the trip.

Geoff had bought a new (to us) van to convert for camping. We thought we shouldn't travel with an empty van, so we told our church that we were going and asked for blankets, warm jumpers and gloves.

The response was overwhelming. By the end of the week we could no longer get into our sitting room or hallway and Mia's sitting room was also full. The word spread around the other churches in town. Neighbours and their families and friends joined in. We filled the van with donations (leaving just enough room for passengers). There were another two van-loads of supplies that had to be sent later.

It is probably a good thing at this point to remind myself of the fear and trepidation we were all feeling. The reports that were coming out of 'the Jungle' in Calais were of hostility and violence. We were told that customs might turn us back if they knew we were carrying supplies for refugees. The van was full of young women, for whom we felt a real responsibility. We had gone through proper channels in that we had booked into a youth hostel and told the L'Auberge warehouse that we would be arriving with a van-load of volunteers and blankets. (L'Auberge des Migrants is an organisation formed to aid the migrants in Calais.)

Fortunately, two of our group, Mia and Frankie, were very fluent French speakers. To some extent, they looked after us!

It was a long journey. We left immediately after church on Sunday and arrived at the youth hostel at about 10pm. We were tired and cautious. Just as we turned to go up to our rooms, two men came through the door. They were middle-aged and British and had just returned from a climate change demonstration in Paris. One look told them that we had come as volunteers for the Calais Jungle. The memory of this meeting has stayed with both Geoff and me. There was no need to explain to them why we were there – that was a given. They welcomed us and said we would get lots of information over breakfast. Suddenly, all the anxiety left us and we almost felt that we had come home.

The girls were full of excitement. They had publicised our trip on Facebook (not something that would have occurred to us!) and we already had several hundred followers and well-wishers.

Breakfast time was incredibly exciting for all of us. The dining room was full of volunteers, about 90% of them under the age of 30. There were a lot of people from universities in the UK, which had just broken up for Christmas. But there were also many young professionals who had taken time off. Some were on their third or fourth trip to Calais.

Over coffee and pancakes we learned the ropes. A couple of girls volunteered to show us the way to 'the warehouse'. We doubled up in the van, as there wasn't enough room – thank goodness it was only 15 minutes away.

After an introduction from the team at the warehouse, I soon found out that we had all been given different jobs. I volunteered in the kitchen, where I felt immediately at home. Mia stood alongside me, chopping vegetables. Most of the girls offered to help sort through the donations, and scattered. Geoff went to the workshop to help build shelters.

We met up after dark and returned to the hostel. The atmosphere was electric. Mia and I had both been chilled to the bone as we stood chopping and peeling in the open-doored warehouse, but we had also distributed meals to hundreds of people in the camp in

Dunkirk, and laughed with the children who came up for more of the fresh fruit and bottles of water we were handing out.

My granddaughter and one of the French-speaking girls ended up at the Jungle with a small team teaching English in the makeshift school. Geoff was working on building a youth centre in the Jungle.

The week went on – full of new experiences. I was quite hesitant about going into the Jungle. 'It's voyeuristic,' I said. 'But they are having an art exhibition,' said Geoff. 'Come and see.' So at the end of our stay in Calais, we stopped at the Jungle. The girls wanted to say goodbye to the children they had worked with.

The Jungle was no surprise, as news reports at the time were full of photos of it. There was mud everywhere and the occasional stand-pipe to wash at. Makeshift shelters had collapsed under the weight of the rain. There were avenues of food shops and pop-up restaurants. And, most impressive, in the middle of this devastation stood a church and a mosque. The church had a tall steeple made from bits of wood and plastic sheeting. Shoes lined the doorway and inside it was carpeted and clean and peacefully quiet. Everywhere people greeted us with handshakes and smiles. Some of the young men wished to try their English out on us.

We had agreed to meet at the van at 11am. As the time drew near Geoff and I started to walk towards one of the exits – marching towards us was a group that looked like a troop from *Star Wars*: armed police with helmets and boots, guns and tear gas canisters. They remained in formation and we had to get out of their way as they passed. They did not look around, only straight ahead. We could see no reason for their being there. I began to panic. I spotted Mia. Where were the others? Were they going to get caught up in the middle of whatever was happening? We did not know what to do. We decided to go to the van and work it out from there. To our immense relief, the girls were waiting for us, surrounded by children and young men they had met. We had acquired a passenger for the trip back. Not an asylum-seeker, but another volunteer, who was going back to visit her family for Christmas.

That Christmas was a time for a lot of reflection. The acts of giving and eating of meals were largely subdued. We could speak of nothing else but the people we had met, the stories we had heard, the volunteers who were putting their lives on hold to help people through this crisis.

We still had a mountain of donations – and more arrived every day. We began to plan our next trip to Calais, but this time we thought we would involve more of the community. We used the church hall and invited anyone who was interested to come and help us sort donations and to share a meal at the end. We asked everyone who came to bring a vegetable to go into the meal.

The day was tiring, but we had more than a hundred people helping us sort donations of clothes and blankets. Some people stayed all day; others gave whatever time they had. We sat down for a shared meal with about 40 volunteers and presented a slideshow of our time in Calais.

Our group for the second trip was slightly different. Some of the girls drove themselves, so we had room for more volunteers; again, they were all young – comparatively speaking. Six weeks had passed and we had heard that there were threats to flatten the Jungle. We could not find room at the youth hostel this time, so stayed in a cheaper motel.

On this trip, we spent more of our time at different warehouses and were involved with the distribution of warm clothes in the Jungle. After the second day, we felt like the enemy of the police. We were stopped at one point and refused entry into the Dunkirk camp. The police were everywhere, eyeing us with suspicion. A lasting memory is sheltering from the cold wind and rain with a dozen young Syrians under a bridge. Parked above were five police vehicles with water cannons on the back. Bulldozers were busy behind us, flattening great swathes of the camp.

On our return to the UK, many who had helped us prepare, enquired how we got on. It was very difficult to express our sadness at what we had seen.

We became more determined to work on the government to get them to change its immigration policy. 'Oh no!' said one of our hard-working women in the church. 'I don't mind sending clothes to them but we don't want them over here!' We were flabbergasted.

After much prayer and consideration (and frustration with the local government) we decided that the least we could do was to try to raise awareness about what it *meant* to be a refugee.

Again over coffee and cake, and with a few more people, we discussed an exhibition that was touring. Called 'From Syria with Love', it featured artwork from children in a refugee camp in Turkey. Mia was reading a book by an Afghan refugee, Gulwali Passarlay; someone else had heard about an author called Diana Darke, who had lived in Damascus. By the end of our meeting we had booked the art exhibition and received e-mails confirming that both authors would gladly come and speak. We were also able to book music and poetry from 'Exiled Artists'.

Our church agreed to house the exhibition and host the night of speakers and music. In a matter of weeks we managed to get signs printed and a promise of Syrian food. We were determined that the town would become more aware of the struggle of millions of people around the world.

Hundreds came through the doors. I saw grown men wiping tears from their cheeks as they looked at the drawings created by the children who had seen so much. One man, opening his wallet, took out a mass of notes and shoved them into my hand for the refugees.

That was nearly a year ago. Our work still goes on.

Our church has given complete support. It is open most mornings to receive donations, and this has brought in many people who didn't know the church was even there.

Our group now has a name: Sherborne Area Refugee Support (SHARES), and we are looking to have a constitution so that we can open a bank account. So far, we have raised more than £4000 in cash alone.

The county council are now on board. Four families have been settled in Dorset, and a first family is on its way to Sherborne. We are actively pursuing more properties for the resettlement of families. The nature of our work now seems to be around providing support for families: translators and befrienders.

Donations continue to come in by the carload. We have now been given a garage and there is a warehouse in nearby Taunton. People from our church and community have given hours of their time to help sort donations. From Taunton the donations go to camps all over Europe and Africa.

There have also been unexpected benefits. One day a woman from another church asked me if I could find someone to teach English to a lady from Bangladesh. As a result we have made friends with a lovely Bangladeshi family. We have conversations in English and teach each other to cook dishes from our respective countries.

We have also received invitations from local schools to speak to the children. For one of these we invited a young Syrian man who brought us the art exhibition. He was delighted to return to Sherborne, and the school has since raised funds for his project.

What will happen 12 months hence?

(To be continued ...)

Iona Community member Alison Phipps/Swinfen is UNESCO Chair in Refugee Integration through Languages and the Arts, and Co-Convener of Glasgow Refugee, Asylum and Migration Network (GRAMNet). Following is a poem she wrote after her time working in the refugee camps at Calais:

### Daffodils

For the first time
the daffodils do not
bring me cheerfulness,
their nodding yellow heads
incongruent, stubborn,
sunshine at the wrong
end of winter.

It is wartime.
The earth wrestles against the seedcorn.
The ploughed fields
may or may not see harvest.

There are old gun emplacements
on the clifftops, looking
across the estuary to
the nuclear power plant.

Around their concrete bases
the same jaundiced flowers.
Spring's heralds or signs of
our fear?

I do not know whether to fight
or to flee. I do not know if the
east wind will spread pollen
or freeze away the first hope of life.

On the borders of Europe they are
herding people into cages and sending them
back to the bombs.

On the borders of this field
there are daffodils, nodding away
as the bodies wash again,
out to sea.[1]

Alison Phipps

Some months later, Penny e-mailed me with an update:

I wanted to bring you up to date with what's happening with
SHARES. In September, we welcomed our first family, from Syria,
into the town! They are the fifth family to be resettled in Dorset.

About six weeks before the family arrived, the caseworker, who had
been assigned by the agency employed to settle the family in, came
to a meeting and told us what the support plan was. He would be
meeting the family at the airport with a translator. If we wished, a small
party could be waiting at the house with a meal. He mapped out the
next three weeks, which would be intensive for the family. They would
be taken by the caseworker to sign on for benefits the day after their
arrival. Later in the week, they would register with a GP; get places in
the local school; set up bank accounts, and so on. English lessons were
a priority and would be set up with an English tutor.

We were really surprised at how well it was planned. Much of our
organising of Arabic-speaking befrienders seemed unnecessary,
though the caseworker thought that perhaps some of the team
could support the tutor.

We got on with setting up the family's new home. Incredible donations came in from individuals as well as local businesses. One of our

Arabic-speaking members taught us a few customs and printed out signs in both Arabic and English saying, 'Welcome to your new home'.

A week before their arrival we were told about the family and that the youngest child had autism. We were given a few details of what this meant for him.

We spent arrival day adding last-minute touches to the house. It was deemed that Mia and I would be there to welcome the family, along with two Arabic speakers. A Palestinian member of SHARES prepared a lovely Syrian meal.

We tripped over ourselves when the car came down the drive; we helped carry their bags, making introductions along the way – at last they were inside their new home!

The caseworker looked around and announced that, as he had an hour's drive to get home, he would be going. He said that he would be back in 10 days.

I couldn't believe what he was saying! What about the translator? What about school? What about ...? So many questions!

He looked at me, bewildered. 'I have so many families on my case-load now,' he said. 'I can't possibly drive an hour to get here tomorrow.'

I asked what the family were expected to do if an emergency popped up in the next 10 days. (I had been assured by the council that a mobile phone or SIM card would be provided by the case-worker.) 'Oh yeah,' he said. 'Could one of you take the father to town tomorrow to buy one?'

We stood there feeling rather foolish. How had we been taken in?

The two people in the welcoming party who spoke Arabic made

arrangements to meet the family in a couple of days.

The father's English was quite reasonable and so this would enable us to communicate with each other. I had recently bought an inexpensive mobile phone, and I gave this to the father for the night should any emergency arise.

Mia and I arrived the next day to show the family the town and to find SIM cards and Internet access for their phones. It was a long, slow afternoon as we dodged heavy rain showers and tried to help the couple with their tired, excited children.

We talked and walked and learned about their last five years in exile. By the time we left that evening, having accomplished our mission, the whole family were feeling excited about, at last, being in the UK.

Mia and I talked on the way home about how we were going to be able to make it work without the promised support. We were surprised at how tired we felt.

Two days later, a translator was provided to register the children at school. The youngest had special needs that were so severe that he would need an assessment before a school could be found. It took two and a half months but that is now underway.

English teachers seemed to materialise out of the woodwork.

Mia had contacted the nearest mosque, and the imam arranged a meeting with another Syrian family, who were settled five miles away in Somerset.

Neighbours have visited to welcome the family, who in turn have shown hospitality to them. Anyone visiting has shared tea and cakes or delicious meals with the family.

My church prays for the family regularly. We all enjoyed an afternoon of soup and Arabic lessons at the church.

I check in with the family regularly, and I've been privileged to witness several events. One of these was on the second day, when I was greeted by their daughter – and received a recital of all her new English words, which were pronounced clearly and proudly. Their youngest child held my hand and cuddled close ... before giving me an enormous bite and pulling my hair! (Each of our team has now experienced some of what the parents have been struggling with since their youngest was born.)

I was there when their SIM cards were fitted, and they were then able to make contact with their family left behind in Syria.

One day the parents told me that they found it disrespectful to call me by my Christian name, as I am a great deal older than they are. Their choice was to call me 'Mommy'. This always makes me smile.

The day the father made his first trip to the mosque (he was taken by a young Syrian father who had been in this country five months), the wives and children all came to visit with our family. As the child with autism is quite difficult, I took him outside to play, giving the wives time to talk and relax.

When I returned some time later there were five Syrian women there with their children! Some had been in the UK as long as 15 years. I was overjoyed that they had all come out to reassure this newly arrived mother. As 'Mommy', I was expected to join them for coffee. There was so much laughter. I left the home buzzing, and with the knowledge that my support role was becoming redundant – they were standing on their own. But I think our friendship will survive.

And my head is still buzzing. There have been so many lessons learned from getting this family resettled. To some extent we were naive. We were very fortunate that one member of the family spoke English.

The great thing is that the SHARES team are planning for the resettlement of another family next month. Our team has grown – in size and experience. Frankie, who was 17 on our original trip to Calais, has changed career direction. She is now into her second year at Maastricht, studying international law. Last month she delivered a talk titled 'Open your eyes about refugees'. You can see it on You-Tube.[2] Wow!

Not one of us has been left unchanged.

*Update 2020:* Our first family has now been here for almost three years. We continue to support them, as getting help for their youngest child has been difficult with the present state of our educational and health services. The whole family now speak excellent English and are first to volunteer when a new family arrives in the area.

We have been through some very emotional times with many who have been resettled here, as they struggle with memories and family lost or left behind. Jobs have not been easy to find and are probably our main focus now, as the men have begun to struggle with boredom and lack of confidence.

Sherborne continues with their amazing support and have now welcomed five families to the town and surrounding villages. Dorset, which had refused to contemplate resettling refugees, now have almost 100 people enriching the lives of so many in our corner of the UK. These people were among the first to volunteer to assist with shopping, etc with the advent of Covid-19 and lockdown. I was told by them that they wanted to give back some of the help that they had received when they arrived.

Geoff and I feel that Iona was key to the work here in our community.

I have worked therapeutically with refugees, including Orthie and his sister Sahaje (who now have permanent residency). They had come to this country from the Democratic Republic of the Congo, on a torturous journey across land and sea.

At the time of their departure there was a civil war in their country; many hundreds of different factions were fighting, using violence against women and children as a weapon. Their mother was brutally raped, resulting in the birth of Orthie and the death of their mother.

Orthie is now 23 and works for one of the charities supporting refugees fleeing from many countries in Africa, including the Democratic Republic of Congo, where, each day, hundreds pour over the border into neighbouring Burundi, also a very poor country, often queuing for up to 14 days without food, water or shelter to get into one of the refugee camps.

Orthie e-mailed me recently about his work:

## Journey to the UK, Orthie

In the UK, sitting in our comfortable homes, complaining about the cost of living or whether to separate from Europe, it is easy to forget that for millions of other people across the world, just to be safe, to have water, food and shelter for your family would be enough. It is just so hard from our imagining, that in our 21st-century life, people are dying because they have nowhere to go or be welcome.

I do not remember my own journey as a refugee; I was only two when my sister and I left the internment camp to be re-homed.

My sister, however, had witnessed the horrific attacks on the women in our village, and nursed my mother until she died when giving birth to me. Then, aged 12, she carried me through miles and miles of DRC's jungle and bush. Had tried to feed me, keep me safe, had endured with me crossing the sea in a boat so small and crowded that all feared for their lives.

There was a time I felt very angry about what had happened. Now, thank God, the anger has moved to the desire to make a difference. I am unable to campaign or take direct action, or even go back to my birth country. I would be too fearful of losing my right to remain – Britain is the only home I know. However, I can use my skills in IT and work within an organisation to support others campaigning for change. It is important to remember that immigration is not a 'problem'. They are real people, frightened for their lives, and needing refuge and respect.

You can read more about Orthie and Sahaje in *The Secret Keepers: Narratives Exploring the Inter and Transgenerational Effects of Childhood Sexual Abuse and Violence* (Susan Dale, Cambridge Scholars Publishing, 2013).

One of the roles I have often taken on, which I feel is very much about justice, is enabling people who consider themselves on the margins to have a voice. This is the role of speaking out against injustice, supporting those who are victims of punitive government systems that process people, often those who have fled in great terror. As Orthie said, for refugees, speaking out is too difficult, and the risk of losing the right to remain or a visa too great.

Bob Thomas, a member from the south of England, spoke to Community members at a Community Week plenary in 2017 about a charity he was involved in as part of his New members project:

## Friends Without Borders, Bob Thomas

I volunteer for a charity called Friends Without Borders, based in Portsmouth. It was set up to support and help refugees, asylum-seekers and migrants. It grew out of a support group for detainees set up about 25 years ago at an immigration removal centre situated locally.

I got to know about Friends Without Borders and became involved when my wife, who is a Spanish speaker, was asked to befriend detainees from South America. After a little while I was asked to do the same thing with some West African detainees who were French-speaking (I speak French).

In April 2015, the removal centre suddenly closed. This was not necessarily a great thing, because we didn't know much about what happened to any of the detainees at the time. Many may have been rapidly deported, some transferred to other removal centres. A few, like the man I was visiting, were unexpectedly released. It left us with a sort of ... not exactly a problem, but a challenge.

Although we had a number of functions when the charity was set up, the main one had been looking after detainees at the removal centre. This suddenly changed to having a single function, namely looking after refugees and asylum-seekers living in the community.

With the closure of the detention centre, the charity lost significant funding, like many small charities squeezed by government cuts. We had two paid staff who we could no longer afford to keep, so the focus of the charity changed almost overnight in two ways: first, we had to concentrate on support in the community; and secondly, we had to turn ourselves into a 'volunteer only' organisation.

So, the two years in which we did this were a bit of a challenge, a bit of a trial, but it has sort of worked.

What I was trying to do with my New members project was not just to describe this process of change but also to describe my reactions to it, how I was feeling about it. Now, I will not go into the full details, but I would like to highlight some of the negatives and some of the positives, because there were both.

Those, like me, who have anything to do with education in other parts of the UK will know about the 'C-D borderline' and quite how important that is for teachers in respect of outcomes. Well, my C-D borderline is that I have three negatives that begin with D, and three positives that begin with C.

The first D is *Destitution.*

It's the biggest problem that we deal with because so many of the folk who come to us for help are destitute. They have no means of support from anywhere – they certainly have no help from the State, despite what some of the media say. Destitution: having no money, no home, no food. It is a problem for a large number of the folk who come to our drop-in on a Monday or Thursday morning.

We cannot give them very much, but we try to give them some food and we try to give them a very small amount of money, which varies between £10 and £15 each.

I don't know if you have tried to live on £10 or £15 per week. I haven't. I would struggle to do it for a day. So, destitution is a really big issue for us.

The second D, *Depression,* results from the first.

Depression is part of life for folk who are in this situation for a long time and just see no end to it. They might have an asylum case that is dragging on for years and years. They can't go 'home'. They can't settle here. They are not allowed to work. This makes them ill. Mental health issues are a big concern for us.

It is also a bit of a problem for the volunteers. Our own physical and mental health is something that we have to take good care of too. Depression is not unknown amongst volunteers.

And the third D is *Discouragement.*

It is government policy to discourage folk from thinking of this country as somewhere they might like to go. The policy is organised, it is deliberate and in a way it is successful because it does contribute to people's poor state of health and poor state of mental health in particular.

So, what are the three Cs?

The first of these is *Compassion.*

The result of the EU Referendum on that fateful day in June 2016 was a terrible thing for refugees. It brought appalling attitudes to light, attitudes that perhaps previously had been suppressed – certainly they were not usually expressed openly. But after the EU Referendum, around the streets of Portsmouth, people were beginning to be openly racist and xenophobic in ways that they had shied away from in the past. This sounds like another negative, but there was a positive response to this among a large number of other people, who responded by rising to the occasion and giving voice to their compassion; and several began to volunteer for the project in different ways.

Some helped us on a long-term basis, some short-term and some simply expressed their support. And that meant so much to us as volunteers, but really it meant more to the folk who we are trying to help. It was a very powerful thing.

So, although this terrible thing had happened, out of it came some expressions of compassionate intent.

My second C, slightly surprisingly to me, is *Constituency.*

I have just got to praise the two constituency MPs, who have done a tremendous amount of work to help what we do – by coming along and meeting people, making speeches and also doing some solid but quiet work on behalf of their constituents. Constituents who have no status, as far as the country is concerned, but as far as these MPs were concerned, they were living in their constituency and therefore important.

My surprise was that both these MPs were Conservatives. I have to give them credit for what they have done. One of them lost their seat in the 2017 election and was replaced by a Labour MP, who has proved to be really supportive as well.

My third and final C is *Community*.

One of the things that has happened in a really positive way, particularly since the referendum, is that we have people from different communities coming together to serve a common purpose.

They are working together to help people and express their compassion. During Ramadan this year, for example, we had a collection from a local mosque. Children gathered a whole lot of food and distributed it. We have volunteers from the Islamic community coming into the drop-in and just working because it is what they feel called to do. No one makes any distinction between backgrounds, faiths or anything else.

The expression of community working itself out for a common purpose is something that is real for us in our work in Portsmouth, and it seems to me that is what the Iona Community is all about.

### Prayer

*Lord, be with those who have no home tonight.*
*Keep them safe, Lord, in your arms.*
*Keep them strong, Lord, in your hope.*
*Keep them close, Lord, in your love.*

*Lord, be with us as we challenge the injustice of wealth.*
*It is too easy to see refugees as 'the problem'.*
*Help us to remember that they are people the same as us,*
*with the same needs, fears and desires.*

*Lord, empower us to work for equality, justice and peace*
*throughout the world.*

Susan Dale

## Sources and notes

1. From *The Warriors Who Do Not Fight*, by Alison Phipps and Tawona Sitholé, Wild Goose Publications, 2018

2. www.youtube.com/watch?v=NfQ64W165PI

Radical hospitality on Iona

Hospitality is at the core of what the Iona Community does, and is good at.

Hospitality, at its best, is a way of *being* towards other people: an unconditional acceptance, a giving without expecting anything back.

John Dale, my husband and also a member of the Community, reflected on this in Iona Abbey in August 2017, following a dramatic reading of the feeding of the 5000 (Matthew 14:13–21).

## The feeding of the 5000, John Dale

What message did you get from that story?

Yes, it was a wonderful, indeed miraculous, outcome – all were fed.

But I want to suggest to you that what Jesus was after was for them to eat with each other – to share food and talk together and to be his 'com-panions'; that is, those 'who eat bread with him'.

Here we have an insight about hospitality.

Hospitality involves giving something of ourselves to the other person – it is a spiritual practice – for spirituality is about relationship.

As you listen you may have to endure another's infirmities – whether of body or character. Hospitality is a call to revere what is sacred, what is holy in each person.

Now, to be hospitable you have to care for yourself by following Jesus' example – did you notice how at the start of the story Jesus was taking his disciples away to have time to recuperate after their work? This practice is well-demonstrated in a monastery, where the monks go to their individual cells for a quiet time so that they can come out into the cloister to greet their visitors. It is essential to keep time for yourself and your closest relationships whilst developing an open attitude.

Hospitality means bringing the stranger into your heart. May God give you the necessary strength and gifts to do this.

The Centres on Iona have, for decades, tried to offer this kind of hospitality to the guests who visit. The Abbey and the MacLeod Centre have developed into places of 'radical hospitality' – where lives are changed. This chapter offers but a few stories from some of the thousands of guests, volunteers and staff members who have been touched and changed by this place.

Agnes was a guest at the Abbey Centre in 2015. She e-mailed me after returning home:

## The work of the Iona Centres, Agnes

Dear Sue,

Hope you are all well. By the grace of God, I am well, and still enjoying the memories of Iona Abbey. I am very glad that I came and was part of the sessions 'embracing change'. I was just at the right place at the right time, and have learnt something. I will keep on reminding myself that difficult times may come, but ... the best is yet to come.

Thank you very much for all your hospitality and caring you have shown me. You are an angel; may God continue blessing you more.

I hope to see you again in future. My regards to all the staff; let them know I had an amazing time and a good journey and arrived safely back home. Bye for now.

Agnes

## Heaven shall not wait, Dora Nyamwija

It is 4 November 2016. Currently I am working on the Resident team based on Iona. A year from now I hope to return to Uganda to be married to Tom, my long-time friend and love, who waits for me there.

I would like to share an affirmation that I wrote a few months ago to encourage people not to ignore doing the things that seem small that are within their reach, because 'small seeds grow into mighty trees'.

This affirmation came to me during a Corrymeela Community week on Iona; we were talking about change.

*Heaven shall not wait*

*We may not change the whole world –*
*but we could make a difference.*

*We shall not wait to feed all the hungry children in Africa,*
*Asia, South America or even Glasgow,*
*and we shall start here and now*
*by sharing the food we have with each other.*

*We shall not wait for border laws to change,*
*and we shall start now*
*by opening our homes to strangers and friends.*

*We shall not wait for the whole world to stop hatred,*
*discrimination, injustice, oppression,*
*and we shall start here and now:*
*through accepting ourselves, our neighbours*
*and spreading as much kindness as we can.*

*We shall not wait to serve God in heaven,*
*and we shall start here and now*
*through serving those we meet in our daily lives.* [1]

This has helped me to understand that I can start by doing what I can, and sometimes, along the way, even what seems impossible can be achieved. I hope this speaks to you too.

Tough times help us to grow stronger. Take a breath, and think about exactly what you need to do in this moment to stay focused and positive. People always carry something good in them; even when we go off in the wrong direction, or do wrong things, there is something good about each one of us. If we strive to see it, we can see it.

Dora was sponsored at a university in Uganda by Danny and Annie, whom she met in Uganda when they were working for a charity, and who live in Scotland. Following university, Danny and Annie suggested to Dora that she volunteer on Iona.

## Volunteering on Iona, Dora Nyamwija

Danny advised me to consider applying for voluntary work on Iona. Tickets and visas would cost a lot, but he said he would pay for these if I wanted to go.

This would be good for my life experience and CV, and would definitely be better than staying in Uganda without a job. I applied. I did not get a placement the first time around.

Danny explained to the Community that he would be sponsoring me, and that I had visited the UK before as their guest, which meant that I had a greater chance of getting a visa.

Later, I got a letter to say I had been accepted as a volunteer on Iona beginning on 15 May, 2013 – which I accepted.

Danny and Annie picked me up from the airport, then took me to Iona the night before my start date. We stayed at the hostel. The route to the hostel seemed so long; it was cold and very windy; I did not like it. I wondered how I would suffer the next few months in this cold climate.

We all shared a room at the hostel, had a lovely meal and the following day headed to Iona Abbey, where I was to start as a volunteer. We were warmly welcomed by the Staffing Coordinator. There was then an induction session, and then we were shown to our accommodation: Cul Shuna – such a beautiful house by the sea. I could see the sea from my bed, and could clearly hear the waves.

I had a great time.

I also applied for one of the staff jobs, and was offered an interview for the post of Housekeeper. Danny bought me a new suit and shoes for my big interview. However, I twisted my ankle at the ceilidh the night before the interview so I did not manage to put on the shoes! Danny came over and stayed on Iona. We had a conversation about the questions we thought I might be asked at the interview. It was the best interview I have ever had, not only because I got the job but also because I felt comfortable enough to be myself.

When I was asked what my fears would be, I said, 'Being homesick, cold and scared of staying in a big room on my own.' The Director promised she would give me a teddy bear to keep me company, which we all thought was so funny.

The Cul Shuna family of volunteers could not wait to hear whether I'd got the job, which of course I told them as soon as I could. They had all been supportive, had driven me to my interview, brought me food, given me ideas on how to approach questions and kept me in their prayers.

I worked as a Housekeeper on the Resident team from 2014 until the end of the season in 2017, when I returned to my home in Uganda and my fiancé, Tom. I have so many memories of this time.

# A first Christmas on Iona, Dora Nyamwija

My first Christmas Day on Iona was glorious – a few people even went swimming. The house party felt like one big family. I had never had a Christmas stocking before, and we made candles and crafts together, and at breakfast Santa brought presents for everyone, staff and guests. This made it even more special, all of us relaxed, eating and spending time together.

A few weeks before Christmas there had been some misunderstandings amongst the staff, and a few people were so upset that they had left. However, kindness, care and love remained, shining through everyone.

I had been checking my e-mails, which I do not do very often. Staff are allowed to have friends or family visit each year, staying at their accommodation. However, due to space being shared and other reasons, we had to send a request to the Staffing Coordinator and also inform the rest of the people sharing the accommodation. I therefore sent an e-mail to all staff, apologising for sending the request late, and letting them know that a friend of mine would be visiting over Christmas. I said that no one needed to worry about where he would stay, for whoever opened their door when he knocked, he would be happy to share with them. The e-mail was a long one, and at the end I said his name was Jesus.

As people read it, they wondered why I had not let them know in advance about my guest, but as soon as they read his name they found it nice and funny.

Most people responded to the e-mail according to their jobs. The Sacristan asked if Jesus would be coming as an adult or child, to know if he should give him wine or fruit juice for communion. The Cook asked if he had any special dietary requirements. The Musician asked if he played any instruments. The Housekeeper asked me to remind him that, for safety and hygiene reasons, he could not come into the kitchen in sandals. And the Shop Manager told me to tell him about late-night shopping and offers of hot chocolate.

When I asked who would be picking him up at the jetty, Sharon, the Deputy Director, replied that 'we needed not to worry about ferries as Jesus can walk on water'.

I enjoyed all the responses. I had no idea when I wrote it that it would turn out like this.

The New Year was full of hope and energy – with lots of games, and people on the island all packed into the village hall, with families and everyone dancing.

## Accessible toilets for Uganda, Dora Nyamwija

I grew up in a school for children with disabilities, and it was always heartbreaking to see children of my age, and even younger, crawling on dirty floors to use the pit latrines, which are just holes in the ground. I occasionally would clean the latrines, but because we all shared the same latrines and there were many of us, they were dirty most of the time. I knew from when I was about seven years old that I wanted to make sure children with disabilities had better facilities, and hoped that some day in future, when I was a grown-up, I would do something to make this come true.

During my second season on Iona, having learned about accessible toilets in the UK, and even having sneaked into public accessible toilets to see how different they were, I started talking to some of my friends and colleagues. They advised me to start raising money and to spread awareness about the need for accessible toilets in Uganda.

Amazingly, people came up with different ideas to fundraise. The first was Elizabeth, a volunteer, who carried out a 'haggis drive' game. It was fun, and people donated money. A quiz followed, and again donations were given.

Sharon, a staff member, spoke to her Iona Community Family Group on the Ross of Mull and Iona, who I did a presentation for, and they supported the project.

Georgina was a young girl from Glasgow, who loved her hair. She also took up the challenge, saying: 'We shall not offer to God offerings that cost us nothing.' She cut several inches off her hair, and donated it to the Little Princess Trust, which is a charity that supports children with cancer. Lots of people sponsored her to cut her hair, and she donated money to the Ugandan toilet project too.

Joyce Watson, one of the villagers on Iona, decided that the challenge for her 70th birthday was to climb Ben Lawers. She did this with her cousin and a friend and said it was not easy, but thinking of the need for accessible toilets in Uganda gave her the reason and courage to continue climbing.

Word about the project spread, and a few weeks later a friend of mine called Angela, who is an associate of the Iona Community, told me that she'd had a dream about reading an article about me and the project in *Coracle*, the magazine of the Iona Community. We laughed about it. Then I said that some dreams do come true.

Angela and I got in touch with the editor, Neil Paynter, who said yes. A few friends helped me to write the article. I sent it off with a photo and it was published. It was after this that most members of the Iona Community found out about the project, and through the Family Groups and as individuals continued to support this cause.

I was also invited to deliver a short session about the project during the summer Community Week, which was about 'becoming change-makers'. After this, more Community members donated money, and we also gathered a team of people who contributed different ideas for the project.

There were many other ways of raising funds. Shalome, the Shop Manager, did haircuts. We had a ceilidh at the village hall with tea, coffee and cake made by the Abbey Cook, Anja. I was invited to speak at different churches, and people spoke to their own churches about the project, and donated money as part of their annual giving.

Cara, an Iona Community member, had the idea of having a donation box outside the Welcome Centre toilets. After the Iona Council agreed, Richard, my friend and colleague, suggested that it might be fun if there was a toilet to collect money for the project. It started as a joke. Later, when I told Shuggie, who is a local and a long-term staff member, he said he had a toilet that wasn't being used; and they adapted it to enable people to put money into it. This toilet box has been outside the Welcome Centre for over a year now and we have got a lot of donations through it.

Caitlin, a former staff member, helped me to create a GoFundMe webpage, and lots of money has been raised through this ...

By the time I went back home to Uganda, we had enough money to construct a set of four toilets, two changing rooms and a 500-litre water-tank, install solar power, buy cleaning equipment, pay someone to help clean, and to show children how to use the facilities, in two different schools. The first was constructed at Tukore Primary School. This is where I went to school when I was young; my mother teaches sign language there and my late father was one of the founders of the school. Later, we continued with the same design and construction for another school, Ishekye Integrated School.

When I got back to Uganda at the end of the season, I went shopping with my cousin Mercy, and we bought the cleaning equipment that would be needed. Many of the people did not know much about the coloured mopping buckets we bought. Several people in town kept asking us if they were for sale and what they were for. We had got them from the biggest supermarket in my hometown; they would normally only be used in big offices or rich homesteads.

I first saw them on Iona. When the children in Uganda saw them they were really appreciative. They could not believe that they could mop without having to bend down. They danced while demonstrating to me how nice it was to have these long mops – much better than using old rags and a basin where you have to bend, which is always hard for children with disabilities.

I learned a lot from supervising this project – for example, that earth could not be transported on trucks when it rained heavily.

It was nice to go to the site, bringing a few sugar canes and chatting with the builders; they were great people and worked so hard, not sure where their next job would come from.

When we went to the next school to do the construction (this school had a few blind people) they all were very appreciative. I remember one of the head teachers bursting into tears, saying God must have sent us to provide toilets, as they really needed them. She said that most parents were not able or willing to pay school fees for disabled children, so even when they had piped water, they could not afford to have flushing toilets.

At this school the water supply had been cut. The well was a long way away, and this was a problem for the children with disabilities; even for able-bodied people it is tiresome to carry water so far. I had to go to the National Water and Sewage Corporation to pay for water so that we could get it for construction.

The project continues and is a registered charity in Scotland. Now we have enough money to construct toilets in another school. I am hoping to go to even poorer parts of the country when I return in 2017. And I would like to hold sessions where we can have talks about the need for accessible toilets even in public places.

I also hope the levels of acceptance and love for people with disabilities will increase, as for years they have been left out, even by their own families. Several years ago in Uganda, they would have been looked at as cursed, so things have improved with education, but I wish it would get even better.

I am humbled by people's generosity and support. Several times I have been in tears, not just because of the financial support but because of the genuine concern that people have, and their desire for the situation for people with disabilities to be better.

## We need each other, Dora Nyamwija

Iona is a very special place, but we all know it is the people who make the place even more special.

Thinking back over my time on Iona, one volunteer springs to mind. He was one of the most amazing people I have met.

As soon as the first group of volunteers arrived, I learnt that one of them on the housekeeping team had Asperger's syndrome. I did not know much about it. One day when we were both working together, he told me everything I needed to know about his experience of living with Asperger's. He told me he liked things done in a certain way, and that routine and order were very important, which he said was because of his condition. I understood this, and made sure he always had proper instructions. I also told him to ask me as many questions as he needed to, whenever he did not understand something. Later on, he upset other volunteers who could not understand why he always acted like this, and wondered why he always wanted things done his way. He would also change things around if they were not done quite in the way he wanted. I understood him, understood them, but did not know how to enable them to get on with each other.

I tried talking to the other volunteers, and I also had a go at explaining to him. I used examples that I thought would be quite easy to understand. I said: 'When you are walking in a group like we do on a pilgrimage, some people are used to walking very fast, others not so fast, but when it is supposed to be a walk for the whole group, both parties must make an effort to get to a compromise so that they are not too slow or too fast!'

I gave an example from work: 'Because we are a team, sometimes someone else may set the tumblers in different colours when you would prefer them to match.' I went on, 'When this is done, do not change them, but when you are the one setting the table, next time, you can match them as you would like. For teamwork to happen, there has to be a compromise; we have to sometimes let people do what they like, even when it is not what we would prefer.'

I was not sure if this would actually work – but surprisingly it did, and by the end of our time together, we had built a team. It was not that everyone started liking what others were doing, but there was a level of acceptance and compromise.

The biggest learning curve for me and the other volunteers came when it was time to say goodbye to this volunteer. He told us how we had given him a chance to work with us, despite the differences and the difficulties he felt that he had caused. He said that he had not often had opportunities before to do this, and this had been the best part of his life.

I looked at this volunteer, and as he continued to speak, we were both touched and in tears. His words were so moving; though it had been difficult, all of us had learned so much from him, and he had also learned a lot from us.

To me, it does not matter how hard we try to be independent, think we can do it all on our own. We are naturally dependent on each other: we need each other; we need each other as much as we need God. This is also because God manifests himself through people. Loving those people we meet in our daily lives proves our love for God.

For more about Dora's story and work, read *Never Give Up: My Life Story from Uganda to Iona*, Dora Nyamwija, the Cloister House Press, 2017, which is available from the Internet.

People who come to Iona as guests, volunteers or Resident staff often find themselves living alongside others with very different faith journeys, viewpoints and life stories. As they work and worship together – and laugh and argue and sometimes weep – they learn from each other, and are often changed by the Iona experience.

Tryntsje van der Veer, from the Netherlands, was a guest at the 'Embracing Change' week that I led at the Abbey Centre in May 2016. In her free time that week she wrote a series of letters and poetry to God – which resulted in the book *Brieven oan Dy/Letters to You*, written in her native language, Frisian, and in English. Tryntsje e-mailed me this beautiful poem from the book:

## The blessing of your eyes, Tryntsje van der Veer

*In the distance is the scatter*
*of the whistling of the birds.*
*I'll look for things that matter,*
*for the meaning of the words.*

*So nearby there is laughter*
*in the blinking of your eyes.*
*It's beyond war or slaughter;*
*it makes us joyful and wise.*

*All around is pain and sorrow,*
*oceans fed with blood and tears.*
*It takes a second to borrow*
*a ray of light to beat the fears.*

*So nearby there is laughter*
*in the blinking of your eyes.*
*I'll care to look ever after.*
*It makes me joyful and wise.*[2]

Tryntsje van der Veer, Iona, 13 May, 2016

## Sources and notes

1.  From *We Bring You Everything, And Tip It Out In Front Of You: New Prayers from the Iona Community*, Neil Paynter (Ed.), Wild Goose Publications, 2017

2.  From *Brieven oan Dy/Letters to You*, Tryntsje van der Veer, 2016. To order Tryntsje's book, e-mail: info@de-binnentuin.nl

Palestine

*The Lord says, 'The land is mine, and you are but aliens and my tenants.'*

Leviticus 25:23 (NIV)[1]

For many years now, Iona Community members have been standing alongside peace activists – both Palestinian and Jewish – resisting the occupation of Palestinian territory by the Israeli Government and campaigning against Israel's policies of discrimination and apartheid.

Mike Mineter, a member from Edinburgh, first visited the Holy Land whilst on pilgrimage, then went back to learn more.

## The Holy Land, Mike Mineter

Why have I gone to the West Bank – three times?

It wasn't the news broadcasts that made me want to go – I'd only heard them present the West Bank as a source of 'terrorists' attacking Israelis. However, a close friend gave me a contrasting account from his time there, and I was drawn to see for myself.

My first visit was fleeting, as is common for many on church pilgrimages. A priest whom I had known since I was six years old was leading a pilgrimage, so I joined him. After seeing biblical sites in the beautiful, verdant Galilee, we entered the north of the West Bank and were driven south, parallel to the Jordan River.

The contrast was stark – this was a harsh landscape of desert hills. Only a strip of land along the Jordan River and a few areas near the road were irrigated enough for agriculture. We paused where Jesus might have been baptised, and made our way via Jericho to Jerusalem. Next day we returned to the West Bank, parked in the underground car park in Bethlehem and were ushered swiftly through

Nativity Square to the churches and back to the coach. Being tourists, our passage through a checkpoint to Jerusalem was easy.

After that focus on 2000 years ago, I needed to return: to respect, listen to and stand with the Palestinians of today.

That happened in November 2016 when I was touched by a Bible study and Eucharist at the Sabeel Ecumenical Liberation Theology Centre – which is about liberating theology from its part in the oppression of Palestinians, as well as living a theology that seeks liberation for all. In March 2017 I participated in their conference and tour, then also met progressive Israelis who seek justice for Palestinians.

What did I learn?

Palestinians constantly invite people to *'come and see'*, so as to *'go and tell'*. I heard of how their faith gives hope in hopelessness; of a desire for *'life in its fullness'* for all in the land, settlers included; of the need to speak and act *'only through a filter of love'*. I was told: *'The oppression must stop, but there is space for all.'* And: *'We can't make a political solution, so we make a difference where we are.'*

I learnt that *'the first occupation was of minds'*: in those who took power, the richness of Judaism was displaced by impoverished Zionism. Israeli politicians had often been *'atheists claiming the Bible for their authority and God as their estate agent'*.

I delighted in the deep-rooted Palestinian culture: the hospitality and humour, the artistry, the wonderful food and drink. In even the most desperate situations we were offered fragrant tea with sage and coffee with cardamom. I was stunned by the Palestinians' steadfastness and courage in non-violent protests – knowing the Israeli response would be violent.

The vindictiveness of Israeli authorities appalled me. I heard of olive trees felled just before the harvest and homes destroyed in winter;

schools demolished just before the new academic year; tear gas canisters fired to maim and kill. I saw an Israeli settlement and its chicken farm served by water and electricity, unlike the adjoining Palestinian town, which gets a different sort of service: *'When we see the drones we know the bulldozers will come tomorrow.'*

I saw how Palestinians are oppressed in many ways. They are cut off from their land and corralled into reservations in the West Bank by the meanders of the Barrier. They are denied adequate water. Their movement is constrained by ever-changing checkpoints, permit systems and road closures. There are middle of the night raids by soldiers; Palestinians are detained without trial (including children). There is disruption of all dimensions of life, through deliberately imposed unpredictability. These actions break international law and contravene human rights. They are symptoms of settler colonialism that tramples on Palestinians' rights. I dream of the day when Israel's energy is redeemed, and put to the service of everyone in the land.

I share the conviction that this is all unstable, *'dehumanising both the oppressed and the oppressors'*, so that a new miracle in this land of miracles is not only possible but inevitable, if we work for it. I heard again and again of how the international community and churches must free themselves from false narratives that accept and collude in the oppression and, through prayer and other action, join in the growing challenge to Israel's policies.

How does this connect to being a member of the Iona Community?

I had joined the Iona Community because I needed to be supported by those seeking the renewal of our churches, changed by people more actively engaged in the struggle for justice and peace than I was, and to live in the connection between these. The Community's members mentored me as I planned my visits to Palestine. The unfamiliar and the extreme then had the effect of stretching me and of beginning to refine my thinking, prayers and action. I pray that this crack opens wide and the Light gets further in. This is incidental, however, and far from the crux of things – which is simply that we fail our Palestinian sisters and brothers unless we offer the urgent support they so desperately seek.

Warren Bardsley, a member from the West Midlands, volunteered as an Ecumenical Accompanier in Palestine/Israel in 2008. Ecumenical Accompaniers *'have four stated tasks: to offer protection through non-violent presence; to monitor and report violations of human rights and international humanitarian law; to support Israeli and Palestinian peace activists; to undertake advocacy work including public speaking'* (from The Ecumenical Accompaniment Programme in Palestine and Israel website: https://eappi.org/en).

Later, in 2010, Warren wrote a book about his experiences, *Letters from Jerusalem: Reflections of an Ecumenical Accompanier* (Church in the Marketplace Publications).

## Ecumenical Accompanier, Warren Bardsley

… It is 7:15am on another hot Jerusalem day. In spite of a light, cooling breeze we know that by morning we will be looking for shade. We arrive at the huge checkpoint/terminal, just 15 minutes from Jerusalem. It is a soulless structure of steel and concrete that exists for one purpose only – to control and process human beings. The way through to the electronic search area is by means of narrow, steel-barred lanes and a turnstile; the so-called 'humanitarian entrance' is for the elderly and disabled, though the whole system seems more suitable for cattle than people.

Today the place is crawling with heavily armed Israeli soldiers and police personnel. If you were unaware of the significance of this day you might assume that the military were preparing for a major political demonstration and expecting a riot. If so, you would be wrong.

This is the first Friday of Ramadan, the most important Muslim festival, and people are converging on this checkpoint from Ramallah and all parts of the northern West Bank in order to pray at the Al-Aqsa mosque in East Jerusalem. Let me repeat this, in case you may have missed the point: the thousands arriving by bus and taxi to this terminal are coming to *pray*, not to make trouble. Some will not be allowed through, either because they lack the appropriate permit or because they are the wrong age. This year, the army has decreed that, apart from children aged 13 and under, only men over 50 and women over 45 will be allowed through. Men between 45 and 50 and women between 30 and 45 may too pass, providing they have a special permit to do so. Many are disappointed, and this year, to add to the confusion, a Palestinian source has indicated that all women over 30 will be allowed to pass. Still, for the first two and a half hours the system appears to be working. The Ecumenical Accompanier on the Jerusalem side reports people going through at the rate of 90 per minute, and on the Ramallah (Palestinian) side the army appears to have the situation under control.

The Palestinians wait, and pass through the first checkpoint with dignity in a place designed to humiliate, women and men filing through separate gates. Young Israeli soldiers appear nervous. Occasionally they move forward to push back the pilgrims spilling off the transport vehicles. From time to time their commander barks orders through a megaphone. The army has created a clear area some 200 yards from the first checkpoint barrier as a way of controlling the flow of people waiting to go through.

The sun is relentless. Still people wait. Two very young children are in the line with an elderly woman; they cling to her, looking up at the soldiers with a mixture of curiosity and fear; an elderly couple, the husband walking with a stick and supported by his wife, move slowly forward. Then a touch of humanity as a soldier takes the woman and her grandchildren from the queue and escorts them through the checkpoint.

What stories are here! An Arabic teacher and his 12-year-old son sit disconsolately at the roadside; he is 49 and will not be allowed past the barriers. Stories are being collected by the large number of reporters from the local and international media. United Nations observers are present and members of Machsom Watch (an Israeli women's peace group: https://machsomwatch.org) as well as the Ecumenical Accompaniers who, together, it is widely believed, act as some kind of restraint for the worst excesses of the military.

Restlessness and frustration build as the time approaches beyond which it will be impossible for people to enter in time for the prayers in Jerusalem. Some are expressing anger when it appears that the army are not allowing any more people through. New orders maybe? Suddenly there is panic and soldiers rush forward, pushing the people back; there is the sharp sound of exploding stun grenades. Two teenagers are slightly injured. Some stones have been thrown by the youths at the back of the crowd, which is separate from the pilgrims. Then, exactly as our training indicated, the tear gas comes and we begin to feel vulnerable. Our team leader rings and tells us it is time to leave. Meanwhile the people on the West Bank side of the checkpoint begin to disperse to pray in Ramallah; there are three more Fridays left in Ramadan ... we may get through next week or the week after, *inshallah*, who knows?

As we all pass through the terminal cage and make our way back to the city, I ponder two questions: What kind of legacy from all this is being handed down to the next generation? And what evil has entered the soul of a nation that will go to such lengths to prevent people from exercising a fundamental human right – to *pray* in the place and after the manner of their own choosing? ... [2]

As Ecumenical Accompaniers, we are called to witness home evictions and house demolitions, to report them to EAPPI and other NGOs, such as Amnesty International, and to be alongside the people involved. To sit with a family in the ruins of their home and hear them apologise that they can't serve you coffee because their home has just been demolished is truly heartbreaking. I will never forget what happened on an early December day:

At 4am on a Sunday morning we were phoned by our contact with news we had been half expecting: a Palestinian couple, Abu and Fawzieh Al Kurd, who lived in the Sheikh Jarrah neighbourhood, were being evicted from their home of 52 years. We knew that Fawzieh was attending her seriously sick husband.

By the time we arrived, the area had been declared a military zone and been cordoned off by a detachment of Israeli soldiers and military police. Members of the International Solidarity Movement, who had been camping on the verandah, were arrested and later deported. The Al Kurds and several other families in Sheikh Jarrah had been resisting eviction for a number of years, first when a group of Jewish settlers from the Yemen claimed ownership of the land. That claim was shown in the courts to be without legal foundation, but the state of Israel refused to re-zone the land. Meanwhile other settlers began to infiltrate the neighbourhood.

On their return from a hospital visit in Jordan in 2001 the Al Kurds found a recently completed extension to their home occupied by a settler family – which, seven years later, was still there. Now, on that December morning, they had taken over the rest of the house. Those to whom it had been home were reduced to the indignity of living in a tent on a neighbour's land.

Their experience has been shared by many. There have been hundreds of evictions and house demolitions in East Jerusalem in recent years, part of a strategy to transform Jerusalem into an Israeli city, which involves the forced expulsion of hundreds of Palestinian families from their homes.

On the day of the eviction Abu Al Kurd was admitted to hospital. He died a week later. Fawzieh now lives with her family in another part of the city, although even there she is not secure. She reflects that she has been a refugee twice over: once in the 1950s when, as a girl, she had been evicted with her family from their home in West Jerusalem following the creation of the state of Israel. Now this ...

As we left the scene that day we recalled her generous hospitality whenever we visited and the words of defiance on the large banner stretched across their verandah: 'We will never leave our home.'[3]

> *There was a crucifixion in Jerusalem today.*
> *Under cover of darkness they came,*
> *long before dawn,*
> *armed to the teeth;*
> *unjust sentence already passed*
> *separating a family*
> *from their home of fifty years.*
>
> *Usual suspects gather:*
> *soldiers lounge at barriers,*
> *smoking, drinking coffee;*
> *friends, neighbours watch*
> *from a distance,*
> *seething with impotent rage;*
> *black-clad religious*
> *pass to and fro;*
> *notable absentees.*
>
> *Some time after noon*
> *a word from the cross:*
> *the indomitable Fawzieh,*
> *wheelchair-bound husband*
> *by her side,*
> *voices vehement protest,*
> *passionate faith that*

*right will prevail.*
*Still soldiers watch,*
*waiting for the end.*

*There was a crucifixion in Jerusalem*
*today ...* [4]

Dr Eurig Scandrett, a university lecturer, activist and Iona Community member from East Lothian, wrote to me:

## The *sumoud* of everyday life, Eurig Scandrett

I sit on a bus on Allenby Bridge, waiting for hours for permission to cross the Israeli 'border' between Jordan and the West Bank, the River Jordan below us polluted, ecologically devastated, 95% of its water having been diverted to the Negev to make the desert bloom. [5]

*Back home, I lobby against EcoPeace Middle East, an environmental organisation that argues for cooperation between Palestinians and Israel to save the Jordan: at the expense of accepting permanent military occupation.*

I watch helplessly as a Palestinian man and his children are humiliated by a bored teenage Israeli soldier carrying a powerful automatic weapon.

*Back home, I teach my students, many no older than that soldier – and possibly just as bored – about the history of settler colonialism of Palestine[6], imagining them in flak jackets and with machine guns slung around their necks.*

We speak with fisher-folk at Gaza beach. They tell us about how the Gazan fishing industry has effectively collapsed due to the Israeli-imposed exclusion zone preventing access to fishing grounds and the attacks and confiscations of boats and essential fishing equipment within the 'permitted' zone by Israeli gunboats. One man tells us how his two children were killed when they were bombed by Israeli aircraft as they played on the beach.

*Back home, we sing outside the Scottish Parliament at a cross-party demonstration against the visit of Mark Regev, Israel's Ambassador and apologist for the killing of these children, two of the 2000 Palestinians killed in the 2014 offensive.*[7] *Our singing is filmed by an activist, and for weeks I'm getting welcome e-mails from friends in Palestine who have seen us on YouTube.*

Stumbling over rubble in the undergrowth in Israel, I encounter the remains of Palestinian houses whose populations were evicted in 1948 and have lived, with their children and grandchildren, in refugee camps ever since. Their villages were destroyed and their land turned into recreation parks, only for Jews, by the Jewish National Fund.[8]

*Back home, I write to the Scottish Charity Regulator to expose the racist land-grabbing of the Jewish National Fund, which is posing as an 'environmental' charity in Scotland.*

I run, as Israeli soldiers shoot rubber bullets to disperse an unarmed demonstration of Palestinians, Israeli activists and internationals, marching, singing towards a village well that has been stolen by illegal settlers.

*Back home, I research more on how water theft is systemic in Palestine, from violent settlers confiscating local wells to major engineering projects diverting rivers, from draining lakes and damming rivers and over-pumping aquifers to the politics of the Oslo Accords, which make Palestinian water management in the Occupied Territory subservient to the demands of Israel – all for the purpose of starving Palestinians of this essential resource.*[9]

I first visited Palestine in 2010, some 150 years after the colonisation by European Zionists, 62 years after the formation of the state of Israel, and five years after the Palestinian call for international solidarity through the Boycott, Divestment and Sanctions (BDS) movement: https://bdsmovement.net. Before 2010 I knew little about Palestine/Israel, despite it being a major conflict that often appeared in our news.

I have now visited Palestine and Israel around 10 times, as an educator, an environmentalist, a trade union representative, a friend, singer, tourist. I have listened to people's stories and witnessed the ways in which the Zionist/Israeli occupation infiltrates every aspect of the lives of Palestinians, and the multiple creative ways by which Palestinians resist colonisation in their lives and in their minds – the everyday resilience and resistance that Palestinians call *sumoud*. In Palestine and, especially, back home, I have made it my business to look for ways to express solidarity in my everyday life – in my teaching and writing, the organisations I belong to, my local community, my creativity, my recreation.

Commitment to justice and peace is ordinary. Every aspect of our daily lives – what we buy, how we pray, our work, the groups we join, the political parties we vote for, our singing – requires choices. Commitment to justice and peace is grounded in the *sumoud* of everyday life: the refusal to accept injustice wherever it occurs.

Hind Khoury, General Secretary of Kairos Palestine, was a guest speaker at the Iona Community's plenary in Manchester in 2016. I was deeply moved by her words, and noted down what she shared with us:

# Kairos Palestine, Hind Khoury

The plan is for Palestinians to be desperate,
then they never ask for their rights.

This conference gives hope.
The hope for goodness and light.

These things are not just something you read or reflect on; they are something we live by every day.

We look together for a spirit of hope that brings out resistance and an active lifestyle, that we can reach these ideals.

We're also here today because we share together
to be the blessed peacemakers and the children of God.
It's also a promise,
and that's why we're here.
You are committed to do more work and ...
this has been a very long cause,
but hang on in there.

I think we always need to go back and see what is happening and what the situation means to us.

I told a young assistant of mine: 'I am going to the UK. What do you want me to tell them?' She said:

*'Hopelessness',*

and it really broke my heart, to hear that from a young girl.

And so today,
the promise of peace is practically non-existent,
with a very adamant Israeli Government and people –
some people –

that they have a divine right
and that we should be expelled, most having to live in subjugation.

In practical terms the Israeli settlement expansion
where we live is becoming extremely crowded.

We live on 11% of our homeland.

Settlement expansion, and land that is confiscated for settlement,
is growing every day and has left us in a poor state.

It is impossible now when we live in our towns,
villages and ghettos for several generations.

I fear for my own children.

I want for them to have decent jobs, to have a small apartment to
live a kind of dignified life ...

it is the reason many young people leave.

There are over 700,000 settlers now living in the West Bank.
In addition, you may have heard a lot about killings,
about young people who tried to stab soldiers
and soldiers killing them immediately on the spot,
and checkpoints.

Most of these incidents happened in the corridors of land between
their settlements, because what the Israelis are seeming to want to
do now, is to join their settlements together.

Another very dangerous sign for us is that we are being terrified,
and one of the policies seems to be ...

'how to terrorise a whole generation'.

The settlements include a lot of infrastructure,
to protect them from the Palestinians:

first-class roads,
highways,
electricity supply, water supply and sewage.

And very often when you visit these settlements,
you find that some sewage pipes,
which are huge ...
from the settlements up the hill
are throwing open pipes of sewage onto our villages.
And you can go and visit such scenes.

On these very old terraces, planted this way for centuries,
they are now being covered in sewage.

There are segregated roads.

Palestinians can't use the roads that are made for settlers,
and we sometimes have to go back, to go round.
It has increased the cost of goods and services.
This is in the West Bank.

In Gaza ...
I don't want to spend too long talking about Gaza.

It is unbelievable in the 21st century that there is
this inhuman siege ...
a horrific siege on 2,000,000 people now,
with no resources. Gaza is practically wasteland.

The people there can't even fish in the sea properly –
the governments of the world say it has to stop,
but what do they do about it?

And that is a very big question.

In Gaza, everything has been destroyed.
The health system,

the education system,
the infrastructure,
the roads,
the school system.

I have not been to Gaza since 2006.
I don't think I can take it.
At the moment,
I cannot take it to go back and see what's going on there.

People do go on though ... they have to go on.

There was an incident in Jerusalem: they stopped all building licences, they closed off areas.

Jerusalem is also under siege
with barriers and checkpoints all around it.
And the difficulty of continuing to live in this ...
outside the separation wall ...
no design, no planning,
crowded ...
Palestinians go and live in an area, because they have to live.

This horrible apartheid wall ...

I have it in front of my house in Bethlehem; they built it across my front door – because I had another door.

I could use the garden door.

And it is a nightmare to live with, this nine and a half metres,
and two metres of barbed wire, towers watching over us,

and guns pointing at us.

The wall has been built to keep Palestinians outside, and inside it is contained all the most fertile land,

the water,
the resources.

Everywhere there are checkpoints.

These are a little easier this year.

About two years ago I remember standing for nine hours.
I didn't go through. I had to go back and stay with friends. Now
the checkpoints are being watched by international observers;
this makes going through the checkpoints less of a horror.

The call, though, is not to hate
but to see through a prism of love.
We need to continue to love,
to look in love as our faith teaches us.

If we love through God,
then God will love through us.

This is the answer:

*Love.*

The love I speak about in acting for justice and peace is not passive,
but active and conscientious.
It pacifies anger and negative emotions and permits dialogue, while
holding firmly to principles.
This is the love Jesus practised and what he tried to teach us.
He preferred going to the cross than giving up on principles.
He was a rebel against injustice,
and he taught us to never give up on what is right and gave
meaning to what we call humane.

If we hate, it consumes us.

But we do need to take action ... now.
Boycott, divestment and sanction are peaceful ways.

A former volunteer on Iona, Susan Lindsay, who lives in Fife, told me about her involvement in work for justice and peace in Israel/Palestine:

## The Amos Trust, Susan Lindsay

My involvement with peace and justice issues relating to Israel/Palestine began with conversations with fellow Iona Community members and associates.

I was on the New members programme at the time, and decided my New members project would be on the concern of Palestine: a country with no freedom of movement and the experience of ethnic cleansing.

I began a deep study, with much reading, and devoured every morsel of information I could on the subject.

Having been brought up in Glasgow by committed communist grandparents and parents, I even attempted to understand Zionism in the light of an idealistic approach similar to communism before corruption. I realised very quickly that this subject was not only massively complicated and divisive to people from the outside, but confusing to Palestinians and Israelis as well.

I chatted with some people from Embrace the Middle East, an organisation whose mission is to *'transform the lives of vulnerable and marginalised people across the Middle East ...'* (www.embraceme.org). They told me about one of their team members who was taking part in the 'Bethlehem Right to Movement Half Marathon'.

My eyes widened and I asked whether there was really a half marathon in Bethlehem.

Yes, was the answer, and this run would help to highlight the fact that Palestinians in Bethlehem cannot even run for 13 miles without having to pass through a checkpoint.

I searched for organisations that were going to Bethlehem to participate, and found Amos Trust still had places on their running team. The Amos Trust is *'a small, creative, human rights organisation committed to challenging injustice, building hope and creating positive change'* (www.amostrust.org).

I signed up immediately and went about raising my minimum charity amount of £1000. I reached and surpassed this goal astonishingly quickly.

At a Christmas party, I mentioned the marathon to a friend, Ana, and before I could count to five – she had signed up too! We were now on our way to doing our small bit for this massive issue.

We went out and did the run at the end of March 2016.

The next day, we visited Tent of Nations, whose mission is *'to build a bridge between people and the land'*, bringing *'different cultures together to develop understanding and promote respect for each other and our shared environment'* (www.tentofnations.org).

I was doing a course in horticulture back in Edinburgh and the visit turned out to be the perfect opportunity to learn more about that, as well as the political situation. Meeting farmer Daoud Nassar there was inspirational. He greeted us with his attractive smile, charming personality, intelligence and (to me) odd choice of a woolly hat and an Arran sweater – it was a hot April day with an average temperature of 30 degrees, with the Mediterranean Sea stretching out in the far distance.

I picked and ate wild, free-growing almonds from the trees, listened to stories about Israeli settlers coming to visit the Tent of Nations, and being warded off – and Daoud's enthusiastic suggestions that I stay and volunteer.

This visit gave me the background to be able to discuss more about the political situation in Palestine, where simply having water is subject to a 'Jim Crow law'.

On our travels Ana invented a new dance called 'the slingshot', which mimics the action of throwing stones using a slingshot. This little dance not only helped diffuse tensions when confronted by the sight of soldiers armed with guns, but also became very popular with the ladies at the women's centre in Hebron (www.womeninhebron.com). It is a hip-swinging, arm-waving little number that best suits a dancer with gumption – and those ladies in Hebron certainly had gumption. There was not a hijab in the house that wasn't flung back with sheer joy as they birled around. This experience will stay with me always; as will the experience of listening to one of those same women, earlier in the day, telling me about how she lost her young son to the bullet of a young Israeli soldier.

When I returned home, I raised money for Women in Hebron, and also for Children of Peace (www.childrenofpeace.org.uk), a non-partisan children's charity *'dedicated to building trust, friendship and reconciliation between Israeli and Palestinian children and their communities'*. I raised funds by doing a sponsored abseil down St John's Episcopal Church in Edinburgh. The view going up was excellent – but the view from the top was spectacular!

By this stage I was obsessed with everything Israeli/Palestinian and even went so far as learning Arabic for six months. I continue to practise Arabic – and I got to use it in my hometown of Fife after I returned from the West Bank.

One of the groups the Amos Trust helps to support is the Alrowwad Centre for Culture and Arts in Bethlehem, which believes in *'the cultivation of creativity as an alternative to violence in the fight against injustice'* (www.alrowwad.org/en). A group of young people from the Alrowwad Centre came to the UK to participate in the Edinburgh Festival. They were phenomenal! I also got to join them for trips out and games of football in Aberdour, where they had host families looking after them.

Being a part of the Iona Community has enabled me to channel my passion for peace and justice into something constructive and has provided me with the opportunity to add to the good work being done by so many members. I embarked on this project with respect, passion, curiosity and love.

In 2012, a group of around 65 guests, some involved with justice and peace work in Palestine/Israel, and some not, gathered on Iona, during Pentecost, to consider a response to the *Kairos Palestine Document: A Moment of Truth, a Word of Faith, Hope and Love from the Heart of Palestinian Suffering*, which was issued by Palestinian Christians/Kairos Palestine (www.kairospalestine.ps).

At the end of the week, the group issued this statement – the Iona Call:

## The Iona Call 2012

We, a group of Christians from many parts of the UK and beyond, gathered on the Isle of Iona in Pentecost week 2012. Under the guidance of Rev. Dr Naim Ateek and Dr Mark Braverman, we considered our response to the *Kairos Palestine Document: A Moment of Truth, a Word of Faith, Hope and Love from the Heart of Palestinian Suffering* (2009).

This is our *kairos* moment – our moment of truth. We are called to respond boldly to the deepening suffering of our sisters and brothers in Palestine under occupation by Israel. We stand in faithfulness and solidarity with Palestinians and Israelis who are working tirelessly for a peace based on justice.

We believe it is necessary to challenge the deafening silence of most churches in the face of the continuing injustice of dispossession and denial of basic human and political rights. We agree with the Kairos document that the occupation by Israel is *'an evil and a sin'* (*Kairos Palestine, 4.2.1*).

Therefore:

- We ask our churches and theological institutions to challenge how the Bible has been used to justify oppression and injustice. We encourage the development and use of educational resources to raise awareness, enrich worship and challenge misperceptions and apathy.

- Palestinian Christians have called us to *'come and see'* (*Kairos Palestine, 6.2*). We urge Christians to participate only in those pilgrimages which give opportunity to listen to the experiences of Palestinians and engage with the harsh realities of occupation.

- We support Palestinians in their non-violent resistance to Israeli injustice and oppression. We endorse their call for Boycott, Disinvestment and Sanctions (BDS) and other forms of non-violent direct action. We call on Christians to put pressure on governments and the European Union to demonstrate a commitment to justice for Palestinians and security for all people.

In pursuit of the above we intend to establish a UK Kairos network, linked to the Kairos Palestine global movement, to alert our churches to the urgent situation in Palestine. We challenge Christians and churches to engage in prayerful study of the *Kairos Palestine* document in openness to what the Spirit is now saying to the churches (Rev 2:7). We must read the signs of the times and act in obedience to God's will (Matt 16:3).

Difficult though this journey may be, we seize this *kairos* moment with conviction and hope. We recognise our responsibility as followers of Jesus Christ to speak the prophetic word with courage.

We are called to respond to the question from Palestinian Christians: *'Are you able to help us get our freedom back, for this is the only way you can help the two peoples attain justice, peace, security and love?' (Kairos Palestine, 6.1).*

Between 2015 and 2017 the Iona Community focused further on Israel/Palestine; this led to the Community issuing a position statement in 2017, the result of informed discussions led by a working group on the subject [10] – and to another gathering on Iona (May/June 2017), with Mark Braverman (*Fatal Embrace: Christians, Jews, and the Search for Peace in the Holy Land*), Hind Khoury, from Kairos Palestine, and Charlotte Marshall, Advocacy Worker for Kairos Britain.

Alongside promoting the Boycotting, Divestment and Sanctions campaign (BDS), the Community has continued to raise issues with the UK Government concerning Palestine. For example, in 2016 a call went out to Community members to consider signing this petition to then Foreign Secretary, Boris Johnson:

## Petition to Boris Johnson

Since the start of 2016 the United Nations has recorded 769 demolitions of Palestinian-owned structures in the occupied Palestinian territories, and the eviction of over 1000 Palestinians from their homes by the Israeli Government and military forces.

In the first few months of the year there was a four-fold increase in the number of homes destroyed compared to the same time period in 2015. On average, every week 33 homes are being destroyed; 11,000 structures are currently threatened with demolition orders.

Demolitions are being used as a means of forcibly transferring Palestinians out of certain areas of the West Bank, East Jerusalem, and even within Israel itself. The clearing of land and people has been used to pave the way for more illegal Israeli settlements and infrastructure to be built.

The destruction of private property is prohibited by Article 53 of the Fourth Geneva Convention.

We call on the UK Government, as signatory to the Geneva Conventions, to exert whatever pressure necessary to stop Israel from further destroying Palestinian property, imposing sanctions if needed until Israel complies with international law.

*From the UK Working group for the World Week for Peace in Palestine and Israel: Amos Trust/Church of Scotland/Council of Lutheran Churches/Ecumenical Accompaniment Programme in Palestine and Israel/Embrace the Middle East/Friends of Sabeel UK/Kairos Britain/ Methodist Church in Britain/Pax Christi UK/Quakers in Britain/United Reformed Church – Commitment for Life.*

*All statistics are sourced from the United Nations Office for the Coordination of Humanitarian Affairs – Occupied Palestinian Territory.*

These actions for justice and peace need continued energy on both personal and organisational fronts if they are to have any effect.

I asked Susan Lindsay why these issues are so important to her, and how she sustains herself in what is often such challenging work. She e-mailed me:

## Peace and justice, Susan Lindsay

I think the issues of peace and justice mean so much to me because I learned about the cost of violence and injustice from a young age. With loving guidance, my grandparents taught me the importance of their values.

My grandpa used to host Communist Party meetings in his house, with my granny providing the hospitality. My parents met at the Young Communist League. Experiencing the Iona Community for the first time, only a few years ago, was like 'mother's milk' and I had a real feeling of coming home.

Politics, the issues of peace, justice and equality, were always around me while growing up, even as an unborn baby. My mum, pregnant with me, would go on marches and protests. I can still hear the chant: 'Maggie, Maggie, Maggie, out, out, out!' Thank goodness my name is not Maggie, or my mum would have had a big shock and the inconvenience of a tiny, black-haired baby en route!

The theme in the family always centred around anti-military feelings, social concern and equal rights. God was something I found for myself.

When I was a young girl, my sister asked me what I was going to do when I grew up. I told her that I was going to go and live in a monastery. In 2013, I did. I met people who shared my ideas about God and I found deep inspiration in those people. My already brooding passion for peace and justice, as well as sharing the love of God, was truly ignited into full flame by the people I worked with in the MacLeod Centre and Iona Abbey.

In my personal life, I have found the best way to heal is through laughter and remaining hopeful, always in the knowledge that I am loved and cared for by God.

In 2012, I was gravely ill. I remember lying in hospital, weary, scared, in pain and alone. The nurse came in and said, 'What are you doing lying there? Are you not feeling well?'

All I could do was laugh. At that moment, I had hope in myself and I turned a corner.

We may not be able to control our environment, our situation or circumstances, but we can remain hopeful and free to choose how we deal with life. On a wall next to the fireplace in the warming house of Inchcolm Abbey in Scotland are traces of Latin texts. One translates as, *'It is foolish to fear what cannot be avoided'*; another as, *'The safest thing is to fear nothing but God.'*

I believe I am safe in God's love. In this way, I believe I share with those living in Occupied Palestine. Because of their own personal hope, they choose an alternative method of creative, non-violent action to be the change-makers the world needs.

### Prayer

*God-with-us, you sit down in our midst.*
*Nothing can separate us from your love –*
*not towering concrete walls*
*or the deep darkness between glaring searchlights;*
*not distance from friends,*
*or despair in our hearts*
*that the world's wrongs cannot be changed.*
*You are with our brothers crowded at the checkpoint,*
*with worshippers far away who hold them in prayer.*
*You sit down in our midst.*
*Born into poverty*
*to displaced people living under occupation,*
*you shared our human lives.*
*To this day, your great love*
*can never be contained by the walls of separation.*
*You sit down in our midst:*
*you breathe hope into the world.*
*Amen*[11]

Jan Sutch Pickard

## Sources and notes

1. Scripture quotations taken from The Holy Bible, New International Version® NIV® Copyright © 1973 1978 1984 2011 by Biblica, Inc. TM Used by permission. All rights reserved worldwide.

2. From *Letters from Jerusalem: Reflections of an Ecumenical Accompanier*, Warren Bardsley, Church in the Marketplace Publications, 2010

3. From 'Stories and reflections for the World Week for Peace in Palestine and Israel' in *Wild Goose Big Book of Worship Resources 2*, Iona Community, Wild Goose Publications, 2019

4. From *Letters from Jerusalem: Reflections of an Ecumenical Accompanier*, Warren Bardsley, Church in the Marketplace Publications, 2010

5. *Power and Water in the Middle East: The Hidden Politics of the Palestinian-Israeli Water Conflict*, Mark Zeitoun, Bloomsbury Publishing, 2008

   'Palestinian landscape and the Israeli-Palestinian conflict', Jad Isaac and Jane Hilal, *International Journal of Environmental Studies*, 68:4, 413-429, 2011

   'Water Nakba in Palestine: Sustainable Development Goal 6 versus Israeli hydro-hegemony', Zayneb al-Shalalfeh, Fiona Napier and Eurig Scandrett, *Local Environment*, Vol 23. No.1 117-124, 2018

6. *Israel and Settler Society*, Lorenzo Veracini, Pluto Press, 2006, and *The Settler Colonial Present*, Lorenzo Veracini, Palgrave Macmillan, 2015

   'The environment as a site of struggle against settler-colonisation in Palestine', Abeer al-Butmeh, Zayneb al-Shalalfeh and Mahmoud Zwahre, with Eurig Scandrett, in Anne Harley and Eurig Scandrett (Eds) *Environmental Justice, Popular Struggle and Community Development*, Policy Press, 2019

7. According to the United Nations, 2,251 Palestinians were killed in the 2014 Israeli attack on Gaza, of whom 551 were children and 299 women:

   www.ochaopt.org/content/key-figures-2014-hostilities

   United Nations Human Rights Council (2015) Report of the independent commission of inquiry established pursuant to Human Rights Council resolution S-21/1

   The Israeli attacks were repeatedly defended by Ambassador Mark Regev:

   www.channel4.com/news/by/jonathan-miller/blogs/mark-regev-war-crimes-inquiry-a-kangaroo-court

   Al Jazeera interview with Mark Regev:

   www.youtube.com/watch?v=rQY4gRoJoPM

8. *All That Remains: The Palestinian Villages Occupied and Depopulated by Israel in 1948*, Institute for Palestinian Studies, Walid Khalidi (Ed.), 1992

   *JNF – Colonising Palestine since 1901*, Mortaza Sahibzada (Ed.), JNF e-book Volume 1, Introducing the Jewish National Fund, 2010:

   www.bdsmovement.net/files/2011/02/JNFeBookVol1ed2x.pdf

   *JNF – Colonising Palestine since 1901, Greenwashing Apartheid: The Jewish National Fund's Environmental Cover-up,* Jesse Benjamin, M.B. Levy, S. Kershnar and M. Sahibzada (Eds), JNF e-book Volume 4, 2011:

   http://stopthejnf.org/documents/JNFeBookVol4.pdf

9. 'How dispossession happens: the takeover of Palestinian water springs by Israeli settlers', UN Office for the Coordination of Humanitarian Affairs, OCHA, 2012:

www.ochaopt.org/content/how-dispossession-happens-takeover-palestinian-water-springs-israeli-settlers-march-2012

See also references under note 5.

10. https://iona.org.uk/2017/10/06/iona-community-israelpalestine-position-statement

11. From *Like Leaves to the Sun: Prayers from the Iona Community,* Neil Paynter (Ed.), Wild Goose Publications, 2013

Offender mediation and reconciliation

Prison was the place I first met Mike, who had been convicted of a number of violent sexual offences many years previously. When I took on the referral, I was apprehensive about seeing him; I had many prejudgements about what he would be like.

He was nothing like my imaginings. He was quiet-spoken, with a lively interest in politics and religion. I learnt, as time went on, that he had had an extremely tough start in life and most of his early years had been spent in the care of the local authority, where he suffered abuse from a caregiver. He had been referred for counselling with me as he was losing his sight (I was at the time running a counselling service for people affected by sight loss) and also because he was preparing to meet with some of his victims, as part of the restorative justice programme. We ended up working together for over two years, as he moved from prison, to open prison, to a hostel whilst on probation, and as he painfully engaged with the enormity of the meaning of restorative justice, and his desire to atone somehow for the crimes he had committed.

Strangely, one of the things that struck me was that (unlike many of my other vision-impaired clients) he perceived sight loss as an opportunity. For him it meant that he had the chance to start again. Because of his disability, he now had permission to receive audiobooks and to have a reader and note-taker for study (he was studying for a theology degree). As a child, he had never learned to read – a new world was opening up that he had never known before. He had lost his sight but, as he said, 'I have gained the ability to *really* see.'

In 2017, Margaret Hart, an Iona Community member in Macclesfield, wrote to me about her work with the Shannon Trust in HMP Styal.

# No bars to reading – by prisoners for prisoners, Margaret Hart

Have a go at reading this:

ehT .srehto eht fo ngis on llits saw erehT
.pmac eht dehcaorppa yeht sa deppots dah gnignis
yeht, nehT .nees eb ot eno on saw ereht woN
taerg a sexob eht fo eno fo pot eht no saw
.god etihw

This is an exercise we use when we are training prisoners who are competent readers to work as mentors with prisoners who have difficulty reading. It provides some insight into how it feels to be a poor reader. Look at it again, but this time scan the letters from right to left – the sentences then appear and begin to make sense. But you need to know how to do this.

It is easy to take the ability to read for granted, yet almost 50% of all prisoners have reading levels below what is needed for day-to-day living. Many prisoners have been let down by the school system, have come from chaotic homes, have undiagnosed conditions such as dyslexia, or have come from backgrounds where aspirations are low and formal education is not highly valued. And the consequences of being unable to read in prison are serious. You may struggle to understand how the establishment works, so fall foul of the system unintentionally. You will forfeit even the little privacy you may have as a prisoner as every letter you receive – your essential contact with the outside world – will have to be read to you by someone else. You will need help to fill in your canteen sheets and menu sheets. You may feel frustrated, worthless, angry and humiliated. You may be afraid of others finding out, and you may find yourself becoming aggressive, withdrawn or a victim of bullying. On release, employment and training opportunities will be severely limited.

The Shannon Trust is a small charity that works in prisons to enable non-reading prisoners to learn to read through a one-to-one peer mentoring model. It was founded by Christopher Morgan in 1997, following a long correspondence with a life-sentenced prisoner, Tom Shannon, in a scheme run by the Prison Reform Trust. Through Tom's letters, Christopher learned about prison life – and was shocked by the poor literacy levels amongst prisoners. In 1995, the letters were published in a book titled *Invisible Crying Tree* and the royalties were used to found the Shannon Trust.[1] The Shannon Trust Reading Plan now runs in 124 prisons across England, Wales and Northern Ireland. Last year almost 2000 mentors were trained and worked with over 4200 new learners to improve their reading skills.

On retiring from a career that spanned social care and education, I was looking for opportunities to use my retirement purposefully – inspired in part by the Iona Community's peace and justice commitment and knowing that Iona Community networks would be a strong source of support in whatever I decided to do. I had been into prisons as a social worker many years before, and more recently when overseeing the Open University's offender learning programme, through which 1500 students studied at degree level whilst in custody. Through this I had come into contact with the Shannon Trust and knew its work was well-respected. So I was pleased to take up the opportunity to become a volunteer area coordinator overseeing the delivery of the Shannon Trust Reading Plan in eight prisons across the northwest, and also a local prison representative at our nearest prison, HMP Styal. The area coordinator role provides an overview across a diverse range of prisons, and the local prison rep role brings opportunity for more frontline engagement directly with prisoners as mentors and learners.

HMP Styal is a women's prison accommodating around 450 people. Many of them arrive directly from the courts on short sentences of four months or less. Others are 'lifers'. The statistics relating to women in prison are horrifying. Each year, 13,500 women are sent to prison in the UK. Women are commonly victims as well as offenders: over 50% report having experienced abuse as children, adults or both; 31% have spent time in local authority care; 25% have symptoms of psychosis; and 46% have attempted suicide at some point. Six in ten women in prison have dependent children and each year more than 17,000 children are separated from their mother because of imprisonment. In addition, 49% of women prisoners report needing help with a drug problem. (These figures are from the Prison Reform Trust, 2016.) [2]

Yet even – or perhaps especially – in such a challenging context, hope and resilience can be found. Working with prison staff in the Reducing Reoffending Department we built up a team of reading plan mentors, whose enthusiasm, motivation and drive is palpable. They have all sorts of backgrounds; one of them has been a classroom assistant, another is a parent of children starting school. They understand the challenge of learning to read. Following training in using the structured Turning Pages reading programme, designed by experts specifically for adults in custody, the mentors recruit learners from across the prison, hold regular sessions with them in a dedicated room, which they have equipped with Shannon Trust materials, and manage a bespoke administration system they devised themselves. Debbie, one of our first mentors, set herself a target of enabling Mandy to read her first book. Mandy came from a travelling background and her motivation lay in wanting to read stories to her newborn baby, who was living with her on the mother and baby unit. Just days before Debbie was due for release, Mandy succeeded in completing the first reader, *Fish and Chips*. They were both euphoric. Debbie and I were interviewed on prison radio and our interviews were complemented by a recorded session of Debbie supporting Mandy in a learning session. The insights and courage demonstrated by the two of them was humbling.

The increase in violence and self-harm in prisons that is reported in the press is widespread and reflects increases in prisoner numbers, reductions in staff, inadequate mental health care and proliferation of drugs and psychoactive substances. Real and horrifying though this is, it is not, however, the full story. I was very moved by a 'vulnerable prisoner' in a male establishment who said how sad he was that all the press reports on prisons stressed the negatives. He felt that prison education was offering him new opportunities, new ways of looking at things and new hope, and that these should be highlighted to counterbalance the emphasis on all that is wrong.

One Shannon Trust mentor writes: *'I tried hard to hide my shame at being in prison. But I realised the prison walls and prison mentality didn't have to suffocate me. When another prisoner told me about the Shannon Trust I was immediately interested. I never considered myself to be educated, so thought being a mentor was out of the question. But before I knew it I met Tony. Over time we built a bond. I could relate to his anger and frustration and help him see past those emotions. Tony discovered new ways to express himself. I could see his aggressive behaviour diminish, replacing his frustration with pride. For both of us, the time we had left in prison suddenly became something valuable.'*

As members of the Iona Community we commit to working for justice and peace, wholeness and reconciliation. We affirm *'God's goodness at the heart of humanity, planted more deeply than all that is wrong'*. We pray *'that hidden things might be revealed to us and new ways found to touch the lives of all'*, and that we might be led *'from despair to hope'*. And we recognise the thin line between the sacred and the secular.

Shannon Trust is not a faith-based organisation, and the language of the Iona Community may be unfamiliar to its staff and volunteers. Yet, like many other value-based organisations, it embodies much that lies at the heart of the Iona Community. Working for justice and peace means building alliances with people from diverse backgrounds, and brings transformation for us all. I prefer to think in terms of making a commitment rather than living according to a Rule and attach huge value to the personal challenge and enrichment that it brings.

Another member who has been working with offenders over the last decade is Neil Davies from Devon:

## Outcasts and sinners, Neil Davies

I came to the probation service in my 50s, having been an Anglican vicar for nearly 25 years in a variety of parishes in Wales and England. I left full-time ministry due to burnout and by a tortuous route began work, in 2008, as a probation officer at Lawson House, a hostel for some of the most dangerous, high-risk male offenders in the country, released back into the community on licence. By dangerous, I mean they were murderers, sex offenders and others who had committed violent crimes. The residents are pariahs of society and often the butt of periodic witch-hunts by the right-wing media.

The two questions I'm most often asked about my work are: 'What are these people like?' and 'How can you work with such monsters?' The answers are very simple. First, if you visited the hostel and entered an informal gathering of staff and residents, you'd be hard-pressed to pick out the offenders. These people with whom I share meals, play pool or darts and meet with regularly on a one-to-one basis to help them reintegrate into the community are ... human beings. They are mostly polite and compliant and, if you take the time to dig into their past, you'll find that they have invariably been victims themselves, of sexual abuse in the case of sex offenders, or of some other violence. Most suffer from some sort of mental illness or personality disorder.

Often our residents feel valueless – because that is how they have been treated by society. The first thing I do with each new resident is to offer them my hand and my first name. You would be amazed at the astonishment this often engenders.

However, I cannot stress enough that this is not to excuse the awful things they have done, or to devalue their victims' suffering in any

way. Indeed, the primary objective of the programme work undertaken by residents is to focus on acquiring empathy for their victims
and an understanding of the effect that their offending has had on
their victims. In some cases, this is quite cathartic for them. However,
for offenders who are in complete denial of their crimes, this is not
the case. For probation staff, these people are the most difficult to
engage with.

I vividly remember two Christmases ago, residents and staff sitting
down together to enjoy a magnificent Christmas dinner provided
by our dedicated, ex-navy chef. As we began our meal, the bells
sounded from the nearby parish church. I glanced around the gathering and couldn't help feeling that Jesus would not have been
down the road with those gathered into the fold at the church, but
would be sitting down to break bread with this table of lost sheep.

I believe all human beings are valuable to God and have the possibility of redemption. When I meet with our residents, knowing the
often horrendous circumstances of their upbringings, another
sobering saying frequently comes to mind: 'There but for the grace
of God go I.'[3]

Neil Davies

Neil e-mailed me after reading an earlier draft of this chapter:

Your comment earlier about Mike being not what you expected
reminds me of my own experiences. In Lawson House, I quickly
learned to avoid reading a person's file (apart from risk protocols)
before meeting the individual. The file, often consisting of reports
written a long time before, invariably bore little resemblance to the
person I met on release. I found reading the files could colour one's
view of them, and this was the case for a number of staff, who
treated the offenders accordingly. I therefore preferred to meet the

person first and get to know the person I met before looking at the file in depth.

I was also struck by Margaret's stories about the reading project. I remember one day a group of us, both staff and residents, discussed what freedom meant for each of us. Most talked about the joy on release – being free to go to a pub or take a country bus ride and so on. However, one old boy who was just released after 20 years in prison, said that the freedom of his release was nothing compared to the freedom he experienced through learning to read and write during the first three years of his sentence. His words have always stayed with me: 'It was – and still is – the most liberating experience of my life.' I have heard many similar comments about the positive aspects of prison from hostel residents, despite all the problems caused by cuts, overcrowding, lack of staff, drug abuse and so on. It makes you wonder!

Justice is often about attitudes, and the way we judge or prejudge the people we meet or work with. It is about seeing people as people, with thoughts, feelings and needs, and not as 'others' or 'offenders' or 'drug addicts' or 'disabled' … The labels we impose on people often distance us from them, yet we all share a common humanity. We are all God's people, and we need to endeavour to meet other people as equals: fellow travellers along the road of life.

The Rule of the Iona Community commits members to account for their use of time and, indeed, time sometimes seems to be the most valuable commodity that we have. Our lives have precious seconds, minutes, days, months and years in which we can love, have relationships, sleep, work, relax and generally interact with the communities we build around us. Sometimes we have choices about how we use that time, other times we do not, but accounting for our use of time is a vital part of what it means to be an Iona Community member. I am fortunate in that I am now able to choose how I use at least some of my time, and often choose to work alongside people who consider themselves on the margins of life.

Lizzie St George, an associate member from Devon, e-mails me about her use of time, which has included work in prisons.

## Following the Rule, Lizzie St George

Clearly one's use of time is partly governed by one's responsibilities. One way I have used my time over the years has been in doing voluntary work. This started in children's homes before I joined the Community and, since joining, it has varied over the years. When my family matured I joined the management committee of a charity helping to rehouse the homeless. I became a Samaritan and supported the Emmaus project near Cambridge.

Then I became ill and had to retire. I moved to Dartmoor, and as I recovered, new opportunities came to light. I trained as a counsellor and did a lot of listening! Running a B&B and a small holiday-let meant I met lots of people, and quite a few of them needed to talk.

Having the holiday-let gave me the opportunity to help a number of women who needed to get away from their current situations.

I was offered the opportunity to help with services in Exeter Prison. Later on, I joined a group that was running restorative justice courses in the prison, and once had the opportunity to help on a course in the women's prison near Gloucester. At this time, I also had the opportunity to train as a hospital visitor with the Chaplaincy at the Royal Devon & Exeter Hospital. I have also always been concerned with people overseas who need help, and a few years ago was very fortunate to be able to go back to South Africa to help in a village near Umtata.

Following the Rule does not just mean 'doing things'; it is more a way of being, of allowing ourselves to be in relationship with others, even as we go about the mundane and ordinary things of life. For example, on a recent train journey I got into conversation with a lady whose daughter has a rare, life-threatening syndrome. When she learned that my second son had the same syndrome, it allowed her to open up and share her anxieties, knowing I would understand.

Whether we work actively within our communities on specific projects or campaign for change, what holds us to our task is our connection through Christ, and to other Community members who inspire and support us in our work, and to whom we account for our use of time, money, natural resources and so much else.

**Prayer**

*Listening God, bless all those*
*who have no one left to talk to,*
*who are afraid*
*friends will reject them,*
*families will disown them*
*and lovers will leave.*

*Bless them with the confidence, loving God,*
*that no matter what they confess*
*you love and accept them,*
*understand their shadow and their light,*
*will never leave them feeling ashamed, poor, alone.* [4]

Neil Paynter

## Sources and notes

1.  *Invisible Crying Tree*, Tom Shannon and Christopher Morgan, Polperro Heritage Press 1995

2.  Prison Reform Trust (2016) Presentation at POPS Anderson Lecture, April

3.  Neil Davies, from 'Outcasts and sinners', *Coracle*, the magazine of the Iona Community, 2013, Neil Paynter (Ed.)

4.  From *A Book of Blessings: And How to Write Your Own*, Ruth Burgess (Ed.), Wild Goose Publications, 2004

Working with our local communities

Many members, like myself, work for peace and justice within their local communities. Most of us do not consider what we do as different or extraordinary. As member Muriel Snell told me recently at Community Week, *'It is just ordinary ... just what we do.'* Often what we do is indeed ordinary. We do what we can, given our age, health and the context and circumstances in which we live. As an intentional Christian community, we bring ourselves back to focusing on the other person, the injustice that is happening, what we can do with others – living out our faith, rather than just turning inwards to our own needs.

Some of the things we do are 'small', like choosing an ethical supplier of fuel or clothing. Some people are able to be involved in much bigger projects. Together, however, we provide an alternative story of living life in all its fullness.

When I became a member of the Community, I remember saying to Peter Macdonald, who was then Leader: 'I am not very well at the moment. I am not sure what I can possibly do in respect of my justice and peace commitment.'

He reassured me that even small things were important.

For my New members project, I anticipated writing and publishing stories with a young Muslim woman who felt without a voice and often invisible. It was manageable. Some six months later, however, I also found myself starting a project to support the local community at a time of crisis, when five-year-old April Jones was abducted and murdered. I wrote in my journal at the time:

*November 2012*

*To 'do nothing' in the face of such distress is not an option. What to do, and what I am capable of doing, I am not yet sure. My Iona Com-*

*munity friends have already started e-mailing their support. I can and will move forward in faith with their thoughts and reach out, even though it feels like stepping into the abyss …*

Since then, I have gone back to simpler things: buying ethically, eating locally grown food (when I can), listening to people and empowering others to develop a voice through writing. Small things, like tiny grains of sand. I hope, however, that every grain of sand adds to others and will together make a difference. I was reminded recently on a visit to Iona that the beautiful white beaches contain many, many grains of sand!

Will Spangler, a member living in Glasgow, talked to me about the local projects he has been involved with:

## Local projects, Will Spangler

I used to volunteer at the Glasgow City Mission, where they offered clinics and day surgeries. It was a place where guys could come off the street, they could get access to Wi-Fi, they were fed, and it was a dry warm place for them to exist without being pressured or attacked.

That was really good, there was good camaraderie; but after a time, I wanted to do something else. So, there was a place called the Coach House near me. This had been there for 30 plus years and run by a retired academic.

He owned the Coach House, so none of the projects based there ever had to pay rent.

Off at the back of the Coach House was a medium-sized shed where we resurrected old tools that had been donated for projects in Africa.

Hand tools, mostly.
And now we also resurrect old power tools.

We used this shed as a workshop
and got the tools all working again.

Although the shed and the Coach House no longer exist, because eventually the owner retired and sold it off, we wanted to continue doing the work, and looked for a new premises.

Thanks to my connection with Aileen (another Community member) and an organisation called Stable Enterprises, we found a little space in a warehouse, which we also have rent-free.

Nothing changed, except we had to rebuild our workshop, which meant that we had to move all of the hundreds of tools and pieces of equipment that had been stored in the shed, collected over a 35-year period.

That was a big job!

Three men and a van ...
It took about a week.

We have now built an office structure inside this warehouse. It has a roof and good light and heat, and now operates as a proper workshop.

It is clean, dry and warm.
The bond of the group involved makes it really important.

All the people are about my age and retired ...
I am actually about the youngest!
When the tools have been resurrected, we give them to a distribution centre, which is in Fife...

They then go to various places in Africa, depending on who needs them. The distribution centre organises who they go to.

We retain connections with two agencies doing that work so that we do not have to get involved in the distribution.

These are Tools for Self-reliance (www.tfsr.org) and Tools with a Mission (www.twam.uk).

Both are Christian groups, but they have different benchmarks for quality and what they might be looking for.

If there is a tool that we cannot bring up to the standard, or is not needed by TFSR, then we can usually give it to TWAM.

That gives us quite a wide scope.

We have done all the tools that came with us from the Coach House, and now we are on to newly donated stuff.

The old tools come in from church groups, funerals, old estates.

The most looked-for by the distribution centres are woodworking tools; next would be mechanical tools. We do not do as many of these as we used to however – the problem being that many of the old mechanical tools found here are in imperial measurement ...

when the rest of the world is in metric.

So, there's a bit of a discordance there. But other things – electric drills are okay, although there's not so much demand for them.

We don't take many of them because we know not many people want them. They are also a lot more difficult to ship as they take up a lot of room, whereas carpentry tools can be packed more densely.

This means that we can send more to the people that need them. They can use them to start a business.

A lot of these people have the drive, they have the ambition, which is really impressive.

We send the tools and they take it from there …

The businesses then help the community by providing vital services.

It is also good for us to work together. I've found that, especially as I get older, I need a focus, to feel a sense of worth that I might not have otherwise.

It was also a requirement of me, when I joined the Iona Community, to do something towards peace and justice, and I decided that this was a good thing that would fit that category.

It is part of our Rule to work for peace and justice and this was the primary reason for doing, firstly the work in the mission, and then this.

It is also fun – but primarily it was working towards peace and justice. That little things can turn into something really helpful. This means that, all of a sudden, the world does not seem such a hopeless place.

If you can do something – if you can enable people …

Certainly, we have lots of testimonials back from people saying how much difference the tools make:

'With this I have been able to change our lives.'

I usually do two or three days a week working on the project and I enjoy it.

I sat with Pat Welburn, a member from York, as she knitted in the common room at the Abbey Centre on Iona. We talked about justice and peace. She told me:

# I can knit, Pat Welburn

I cannot be quite as actively campaigning now, but I do what I can.
For example, I can knit.

I go to the local charity shops and buy the wool they sell.
Then I knit the wool into hats,
and then I give these back to different charity shops.

They can then sell them and make a profit.
It is a small thing
but I think perhaps it helps in a small way!

What we do for justice and peace is often intrinsically linked with our personal experiences, where we are living and what we do as a job. Mike Holroyd, a member living in Edinburgh, e-mailed me with a reflection:

# Dancing on the edge, Mike Holroyd

I remember reading, many years ago, a book by Richard Holloway (previous Bishop of Edinburgh) called *Dancing on the Edge* (Font, 1997). The book contained much helpful thought and reflection on issues of faith and society – still as relevant today as it was over 20 years ago. But, more than anything, the title has stayed with me because, in no small way, it reflects who I am and where I find myself.

I identify both as a disabled person, by way of being registered as blind, and as a gay man. These two characteristics do not define who I am but they are important aspects of my identity. So for me, as with many, my passion for peace, justice and wholeness have been intrinsically linked with my own personal experience. This is, of course, a blessing and a burden. A blessing because personal experience can bring such a rich perspective in a world of ideas and theories; a burden because it is easy to feel that one is not really committed to peace, justice and wholeness unless it is purely altruistic – perhaps a rare achievement in any case.

As a disabled person, I worked for many years in the arena of advocacy, and latterly advice and management. It was during this work in particular that I began to question my own understanding of peace and justice with regard to the Rule of the Iona Community. As an aside, the word 'rule' has never worked for me – perhaps because I associate it with 13 years of life in a boarding school from the age of five, where rules commanded fear, conformity and containment. Only very occasionally, in my case, did rules provide an opportunity for boundary-pushing and daring discovery – and I was always the one who was caught! My advocacy work was very powerful in helping others to have or find a voice. I had spent many hours assisting people with expressing their needs, arguments and complaints. There is, no doubt, a need for advocacy, never more so than in our current society, which works on the principles of scarcity rather than the grace of abundance.

But where was the peace? So many people I supported, whilst having perfectly reasonable requirements, would live their days consumed with a particular issue or problem, reluctant to let it go. And even if one problem was resolved, another would soon materialise, needing at least as much energy as the first. It became clear to me that justice without peace is at best ineffectual, and at worst dangerous.

Many of us seek justice, whether in our own lives or in the wider life of the world, in order to achieve a sense of peace. If only we get this or that sorted, then we will be able to enjoy a greater sense of peace. However, I have come to realise that peace is first and foremost a work of the soul, and not of the campaign or placard.

The acceptance of myself as a gay man has not been without its trials and tribulations. Like so many, my formative experience of Christianity had been conservative in its treatment of gay people. It was just about all right to be gay in most circles, but not all right to be obviously or actively so. I read and talked, and talked and read for years, sometimes achieving a sense of self-acceptance, only then to engage in further reading or conversation that once again ate away at the foundations beneath me. Arguments about justice, psychology, scriptural interpretation and situational ethics were never ultimately going to be the things that led to my self-acceptance. These things provided a framework and perhaps, in the borrowed words of Richard Rohr, *'a lever and a place to stand'*[1]; but they would never bring long-lasting resolution. It is the knowing of the heart that has finally enabled me to accept myself for who I am. It is the place where I am required to 'not just do something' but 'stand there'; the place beyond 'when all is said and done' – the place of peace.

It is these particular dimensions of personal experience that have informed and strengthened my work in both the disability sector and my pastoring in LGBT+-affirming churches. In my own experience, my effectiveness in the arena of justice has been directly proportional to my own sense of inner peace. Perhaps peace is where our souls connect most deeply, and the place in which we recognise the beauty of the other and allow it to be reflected back into ourselves. Certainly, I am more of a contemplative than an activist; I am more comfortable creating and participating in inclusive worship than I am marching for justice – although I have done both. And this is where community is so important. We need the contemplative and we need the activist; and the lack of either and the lack of respect for either diminishes us. But if we allow the contemplative and activist to grow together, we journey into a place of wholeness where the divine purpose of the universe is set free to bring about the healing of the nations. Justice without peace generally gives birth to more anger, more bitterness. Peace without justice quickly becomes introspective. Peace and justice together open up sacred spaces where dreams and visions can be gracefully nurtured into a new reality.

On Iona, at Community Week 2017, I asked Jean Belgrove, from Fleet, why being a member of the Community was important to her, and what she was doing for justice and peace:

## Empowering others, Jean Belgrove

Twenty-three years ago, I was looking after my husband who was ill. I was exhausted; it was a nightmarish situation. I felt really broken mentally, not really coping with the situation.
The priest in the next parish knew of me.

He said he was coming up to Iona, and would I like to come?
And I came then, and many, many times after that.

Over the last 20 years, I have come to Iona numerous times.

What actually helped me greatly was that when I knew my husband had his brother to look after him for a few days, maybe a week, I was free to phone the Iona booking office. It might not even have been from a Friday to a Saturday, as it is now, and they always welcomed people.

If they didn't have room, they made room.

One time, I remember arriving at 6pm at the end of the track to Camas (the Centre on Mull).

You were tipped off the bus there.
I had no idea where Camas was;
I didn't really know what it was.

But I got off the bus and I started walking.
I didn't know which way to go …
because at the beginning of the track
you could turn left, or you could go along the boards.

Anyway, I had a haversack, and I thought,

'Let's go for the boards.'

Eventually I got there.

They were so welcoming, and the dormitories were full,
but they knew I was coming and they allocated me one of the sheds
where the volunteers sometimes stay.

It was totally empty except for a chair and a sleeping shelf with mattress and pillow.

I always carried a sleeping bag in those days.
And I just slept and slept and slept.

I could hear the sea.
I could hear the birds.
I could hear chatter.

I joined in with the chores and making bread, I seem to remember,
they were so …

They just allowed me to be me.

And it was not in my culture in those days.
It was not in the situation I was in at home.

I went for a long walk. Goodness knows where … beautiful bays.
I had no idea where I was …

I just walked and walked and walked. But it was just what I needed.

But then, okay …

How do I get back? I found lots of little tracks. It did not occur to
me that they were sheep tracks. They did not go anywhere!

Eventually, however, I saw the fence of the main track that I had walked along the previous evening. So, I got back and it was fine and lovely, but ...

there was no, 'gosh, you are late' or that.
They were confident and caring ...

It was so lovely.

Other times I would be put into Abbot's House on Iona.

Again, I could sleep.

I didn't join in programmes, but came for the meals and joined in with the chores. This helped me so much.

On leaving Iona in those days I used to stay at one particular B&B for one night in Oban and the following day would walk from Oban to the Kerrera ferry point to take me over to the island. Walking around the whole island enabled me to 'step' from one way of life to another.

In those days it was grazed by black sheep – I had an affinity with the black sheep!

It helped me – like a stepping stone.

To go back ...

So, when I got to 70 I wanted to give the Community something back and I decided to return and volunteer.

I said on the form I would like to be in the Abbey, and I sat in the Chapter House, and they said,

'Yes, Jean, you are going to be in the MacLeod Centre.'
And I thought, 'Okay, Lord. What else do you want of me?'

And I loved it.

It taught me transforming negativity to positivity.
That was very good.

It taught me to work as part of a team. I had been a mother with three sons, a very powerful and caring husband and we also 'walked beside' two extra boys. I was in a male-dominated household.

To work as a team was completely alien and being at the MacLeod Centre, I realised the benefit of teams.

Well, I just loved every moment. I was in housekeeping for six weeks. For me to do the high bunk beds was tricky, but there were plenty of toilets/bathrooms and showers to keep me busy!

I loved it when the guests came in, especially the children. Some of them had no idea what to do, had never eaten homemade bread and vegetables …

By Tuesday they did it; we had not told them what to do; we hadn't lectured them. They learned by example, and they were passing the food and eating everything that was given to them.

The sharing was important, and example rather than lecturing.

So that was another big lesson. I decided that the way I live is very important. When I went back I started to live the Iona Community Rule. Not officially.

I had been an associate for many, many years and I had got to the situation locally where I was feeling like a round peg in a square hole. I had a lot of friends in the area and I was very active in the church, with the youth, and had a home group, but it just didn't feel right.

So, I thought … Iona Community.

I wrote to the Leader, Peter, and explained.

Had the interview and went to Camas again.

I was accepted – I felt very blessed.

And I got to the end of the track at Camas and I thought, 'What am I doing? I am 72 years old on a two-year probation course.'

But it soon dissipated – and again, I just loved Camas and it reinforced working as a team.

It reinforced that I was with like-minded people, part of a new team getting to know people, where I know people very well and they know me. So that was a fresh approach.

I observed a lot …

I observed Peter, the Leader of the Community, who went to carry the litter to the end of the track. He was also the one who would get to the sink really fast and start washing up.

And I thought,

'With a leader like that – I can follow.'

And living the Rule at home, and being part of the Thames Valley Family Group, I just became happier and happier.

I had been right through my house and got rid of anything that I didn't need, except what I want to leave for my family.
My house is much simpler to live in now.

All of the spare beds are made in case anyone wants to come and stay; my garden is now completely eco – no insecticides and things.

And it is beautiful.

The garden is quite small, but my sons made me a big box in which I can grow an enormous amount of the food, which I eat. The example in Camas: to go out in the morning and collect what is available and bring it back – that is what you are going to eat.

That is amazing! The meals you can create from that.

I have always been interested in craft, but I have noticed a lot of people making and creating things here on Iona. So, at home we have now got a craft group up and running. We make all sorts of things.

At the moment we are making angels and they are going to go to every child who comes to the church at Christmas; and Churches Together in Fleet is very strong, so everyone is making angels, in all of these churches. We are also going to give them out in the shopping precinct with a little text.

One big thing that has enabled me to do more is good husbandry of time. I did the good husbandry of my house, my money, and now also my time.

People tended to ask me, 'Can you do this?' or 'Can you do that?' And I would do it. Well now, I sometimes say no, but I get up early and have prayer time, then go on the computer until the e-mails are done.

Probably I spend about an hour for that day's e-mails, then the computer goes off until the next day. People now know that if they want to contact me in the afternoon I will not open the computer until the following day.

It's enabled me to talk to a lot more people, really communicate to a lot more people.

Making time for my family is very important too. When I was 70, I brought them all up to Iona for my birthday. My first-year project for the New members programme was connecting with my community.

So, the first thing I did …

we had no buses because the government had cut the subsidies – so therefore, I joined Transition Town on their committee who were interested in promoting sustainable public transport.

Now, I am not very computer-savvy but the younger ones were. But I did things like leaflet-dropping. I stood on the pavement with a placard.

We needed the buses, and a lot of people were mumbling and grumbling but not doing anything about it.

To cut a long story short – we now have two bus services, one going around Fleet every half an hour and one going from Reading to Fleet to Farnborough.

The next thing we needed was to get people from Fleet to Frimley Park Hospital, which was difficult because of parking difficulties. So what we did was to set up a meeting with the press.

We travelled to the hospital. One group of people got on the bus service that existed – you went from Fleet to Farnborough, then changed buses and so on. And one group of the people walked the seven miles to the hospital. And, luckily, the group that walked got there first!

And we got the press coverage for that. It demonstrated the problem! We have not got the bus service there yet – but we are hoping …

I read in *Coracle* (the Iona Community's magazine) that markets were extremely good places to buy food, especially local farm markets with fresh vegetables.

Well, we have a young couple who are trying to start a community farm so – I tried to encourage them, and the farmers' market stopped because they said that there was just 'not enough footfall to make it worth their while'.

So I wrote to all the parish councillors and said, 'Look, the farmers' market has stopped coming. Could we not have our own market for local businesses so that we can stop this ridiculous practice of flying food in from all over the place?'

And one parish council took it up and they gave us a six-month trial.

They put in a manager and that gave me the opportunity to encourage her, and for me to find ways of being a 'bridge' bringing people to the market. I was leaflet-dropping like mad! Taking car-loads of people up to the market.

And that was reasonably successful, and we were given another six months. So again, leaflet drops, notes in the parish magazine, so that is now ongoing.

The market is there to stay.

Now … I was a street angel until I was 70 but that was between 10pm and 3am, so at 70 I decided to help instead at the young people's disco. We are allowed 750 teenagers, who take over the Harlington Centre.

There is a disco, a quiet room, a tuck shop, a cloakroom, and all the money raised goes towards youth work within Fleet. So, we were able to buy musical instruments for some children who couldn't afford music lessons, and provide instrumental lessons free. There were also several projects offered during the holidays. They also run activities for the children in the park as well.

But again, teamwork – the police are involved, the Lions Club, St John's Ambulance, the churches and youth workers are involved; and some of the youth are doing their Duke of Edinburgh awards and their Community badge.

I can remember, at the start, the disco meant us running backwards and forwards checking the cloakrooms and so on, but now it is much more setting it up and the youngsters do the running around.

It is often about empowering others. I have learned that my task is about empowering, encouraging and enabling others.

### Prayer

*Hold us, O God, with your hand;*
*not simply because we yearn for security*
*but so that we may be guided in unfamiliar places.*

*Touch us, O God, with your embrace;*
*not simply because we yearn for your intimacy*
*but so that we may embrace others with your compassion.*

*Carry us, O God, in your arms;*
*not simply because we cannot walk alone*
*but so that we may have the strength*
*to carry the burdens of those around us.*

*And as you hold, touch and carry us,*
*lead us deeper into your presence because,*
*when all is said and done,*
*presence is all there is,*
*and presence is all that we can be.*

Mike Holroyd

## Sources and notes

1. *A Lever and a Place to Stand: The Contemplative Stance, the Active Prayer,* Richard Rohr, HiddenSpring, 2011

Cutting the carbon: Walking softly across the earth

*We stand and watch what remains of an orange-red glow*
*Slipping gently through a gap between sea and clouds*
*Past the edge of the sea as clouds shift to change its final shape.*
*Our eyes cannot hold its gaze for long.*

*The infectious silence breaks with a sigh as the last ember winks out*
*Which betrays our knowing that the sun will rise no more to our cry.*
*Then God will change for our latest whim.*

*Earth turns in the light and we who stand see the beauty no more.*
*We too must turn and be warmed by the light that continues on.*
*To wait and to see once again of the beauty and brightness*
*That once delighted us.*

Written by associate member Stuart Elliott for the Greenbelt Festival, 2014 [1]

The Iona Community's commitment to '*justice, peace, wholeness and reconciliation*' applies also to members' interaction with the natural world and how we use the earth's resources, including how much gas and electricity we use to power our homes. It also looks at personal travel. The growing international debate about climate change has led many members to proactively working to reduce their own carbon footprint and that of the communities in which they live, and also campaigning on national and international fronts.

My introduction to the effects that human activity and pollution could have on the environment and the climate – and a realisation that how we as a society use resources needs to change – came in the late 1970s when I visited the Centre for Alternative Technology in Machynlleth in mid-Wales. This was an inspiring community of pioneers developing new ways of creating power. Radically, they were suggesting that as we burned what would become rare fossil fuels to power our houses, workplaces and transport systems, we were creating toxic carbon, which was effectively burning a hole in the ozone layer that protects the Earth from the sun's rays. They warned that unless we halted, and rethought our priorities and ways of living, the earth would warm up, which would result in our weather becoming more volatile, droughts, the pack ice in the polar regions melting, sea levels rising dramatically and floods, meaning that much of the ecosystem and many countries would not be able to sustain life.

They were seen as 'eccentric hippies', but at the time – as I walked around their visitor centre, played with the first solar panels and wind turbines and looked at ways of recycling waste – I remember feeling a certainty that these were issues that could not be laughed off or ignored.

Some decades later, in 2008, we came to live in Machynlleth. Our retirement cottage, Bron-yr-Aur, was nestled high in the hillside above the Centre for Alternative Technology – not so alternative now, with many people concerned about climate change, and the landscape becoming dotted with wind and solar farms.

Bron-yr-Aur was an old shepherd's cottage surrounded by sheep and Forestry Commission land. It had no electricity, lighting or water heating. Since the 1960s, cooking had been done by gas, heating by way of a large inglenook fireplace and local wood, and water was piped from a tank in a nearby stream. The walls of the cottage were thick stone, the floor flagged in local slate. We were not granted permission to have electricity poles so were unable to connect to the mains. My husband, John, started to investigate how we could still make the cottage viable for us to live in on a full-time basis (previously we had just used it as a holiday retreat). He remembers:

# Bron-yr-Aur, John Dale

Living at Bron-yr-Aur was harder than I had ever imagined. When summer gave way to one of the coldest winters the UK had experienced it struck me that living without the modern convenience of on-tap amenities was just hard – and relentless. That cold grey winter gave us no sun for our solar panels, no wind for our turbine – we had not at that time installed a water turbine – so very soon we ran out of power, and our trusty generator, which had started so eagerly during the warm summer months, would not now start. It did not like the cold weather, and needed to be pushed and dragged into the house overnight to stop it seizing up. That first winter, our water supply also froze, meaning that to have water for cooking and such basic things as flushing the toilet, we had to carry water uphill from the stream.

Our central heating and hot water, provided by a very 'green' wood-pellet boiler, also required a certain amount of power to keep the auger turning, and water such that it did not overheat. So, soon into the freezing weather, we were back to gas lamps and the wood fire that consumed wood at an alarming rate and soon left our woodshed depleted. Welcome to living sustainably – it was hard.

The grey slate rock and abundance of wildlife meant that growing food for ourselves was always challenging; a large polytunnel and several tons of manure helped. Our son-in-law and daughter, who now live at the cottage, are much more successful in this respect, and indeed more resilient than we were. We found ourselves for the first time often without the means to warm ourselves, travel, and cook or wash at the flick of a switch – a lifestyle many in the world live with all the time. Our teenage daughter learned very quickly that, even on a summer's day, if she used the hairdryer, it may mean there was not enough electricity for television; or if I used the washing machine, I could not vacuum the carpet. Unless of course it was a sunny, windy day, in which case there was an abundance of hot water for showers, the washing machine, vacuuming and even the dishwasher. However, using all of these at the same time would inevitably overload the system, at which point the fuse would blow and we would again be without power.

The years spent at Bron-yr-Aur gave both myself and John a huge regard for resources such as heat, light and water, which we take for granted in our 21st-century Western world but the securing of which was an everyday struggle for the people who lived in and farmed this land in previous centuries. They were definitely hardier folk than me. What I also learned, however, was that reducing the carbon we produce and treating the world more respectfully is not just about cutting back on our flights to exotic far-off places or turning down our heating a bit, but involves a whole lifestyle change; and that this is possible when we are young, fit and able but becomes harder if we become unwell or are disabled in some way, and unable to cut the necessary wood, climb down to unclog stream-water systems and drag generators backwards and forwards. It becomes almost impossible in a world where extended families are unable to help, because they live spread across the world. Even now, living in a modern home where the lights come on at the touch of a switch, I am aware of my blessings and the power I have within my Western lifestyle to make different choices. I am thankful and, hopefully, respectful of what I use, but I also recognise that this is not enough. Much bigger cultural changes are needed throughout the industrialised world if we are to be serious about combating global warming. This will take considerable commitment and a change in societal and educational values.

## Community initiatives

When John and I joined the Iona Community, John took on the role of Carbon Coordinator for the Community as his New members project. For two years, members used an online carbon calculator to consider their household usage of power and modes of travel, and to account for this to fellow members. We also calculated how much carbon the Community produced in its organisational activities. The point was not to see who could have the lowest carbon score, of course, but to raise our awareness of how we use the earth's resources and of the value we put on them. John wrote in the Community's magazine, *Coracle*: [2]

# Our carbon, John Dale

We are called on to conserve natural resources and to act caringly and lovingly towards all our neighbours. How we exercise this role and enormous responsibility can be shown in many ways. We can express our concern about the depletion of the ozone layer, the melting of the ice caps and the emission of greenhouse gases by lobbying politicians and by looking carefully at our own lifestyle choices. How we do this within the Iona Community is understandably manifold. The purpose of carbon accounting is to raise awareness of where carbon emissions come from in our daily lives, to account for them and to identify what can be changed at individual and political levels. This should be seen as part of our collective commitment to action for justice and peace.

I believe that Christians are called to be a prophetic voice on climate change. Our actions impact on people across the world and, as Christian Aid has pointed out: *'It is the communities who are most vulnerable and least able to protect themselves who are suffering the most. Politicians will only take action when they see how much we really care.'* [3]

I asked a number of members why and how they wrestle with these issues. Richard Sharples, a Methodist minister, wrote:

## A low-consumption lifestyle, Richard Sharples

As a family, we are committed to a simple, low-consumption life-style, which includes using a push lawn mower, living without a car, holidaying by public transport where we can and eating a largely vegetarian diet.

Looking back over the last eight years is interesting. The choice to go without a car has been the most significant element that has shaped our lives and lifestyles and my ministry. It means that there are some things that I cannot do and that I naturally operate in a more interdependent way (accepting lifts to meetings, for example, and all the conversations that take place on the way). It has shaped my world view, including an awareness of local bus services, although most of my travel is by bike. Cycling builds space and exer-cise naturally into my day, and I have found a way of praying as I go – giving thanks to God and saying hello to the day. Not having a car consistently provokes conversation, which means it is a very good witness.

One of the other key elements that has emerged during our time in Wrexham has been hospitality. We have shared our family home with four young men over the years: one roofless man from Wrexham; one teenager from Iraq; one man seeking asylum from Eritrea; and, currently, a young Kenyan student who has become adopted family. Such a practice has shaped not only our lives but also the world view of our three teenage daughters.

In terms of our carbon footprint, in addition to the actions I have described, we have arranged relatively simple energy-saving meas-ures around the house: draught-proofing, loft insulation and a solar thermal panel on the roof. We have encouraged the Circuit to install new double-glazing throughout the manse and have switched our supplier to one with a commitment to fairness.

Recently, our youngest daughter, Eve, has enlightened and challenged us concerning the impact of animal agriculture. It is *the* greatest contributor to climate change, far beyond energy generation and travel. We eat primarily vegetarian in any case, but now Eve has turned vegan and Mary, one of my other daughters, has become fully vegetarian. My wife, Biddy, has, for many years now, operated an informal consumer co-op around Suma deliveries, so that we get a lot of food delivered in bulk and other people pick up their orders from our garage. She also orders regularly from Traidcraft. So our visits to the supermarket are occasional and for a limited list of goods.

David Osborne, a member from Somerset, writes in his book *Love for the Future* (Wild Goose Publications):

## Love for the future, David Osborne

To respond as a society and as individuals to the ecological crisis, we need an understanding of what is happening and we need technological innovation. These are crucially important. We need the skills, the energy and the equipment. But we also need suitable attitudes. We need to be able to face up to what is happening. And having done so, we need to be able to deal with the fears, frustration and sadness we feel. We need to be able to assess possibilities, and make changes, to avoid being paralysed or debilitated by what we know is happening or the fear of what might happen. Our survival and the health of life on the earth depend not just on ideas and technological changes but also on our attitudes, and on finding the mental and spiritual resources to be able to deal with what is happening.[4]

David's book provides such resources. He e-mailed me, saying:

I think responding to the ecological crisis is a matter of spirituality as well as action, inwards as well as outwards, what we are and become as well as what we do. That's very big and broad-brush but it can work out in small things. Take the matter of our carbon footprint.

We need to try to keep our carbon footprint as small as possible, and reduce it further if we can. The first thing has been to look at what it is, and work out the different aspects of our lifestyle that cause carbon emissions. To do that you can use a carbon calculator (there are several of these on the Internet). The two big things causing carbon are likely to be transport and heating the house. There will be other stuff as well, such as the corporate areas like the carbon footprint of the place we work and our local community – refuse collection, medical, police and rescue services, social care and so on. These can only be addressed by being involved in management or local politics, which may or may not be something that people are interested in. But even if we are not, all of us still have a vote in who is elected and we can think about what kind of priority the party we support gives to the environment.

There are also simple things we can do, like keeping an eye on our appliances and not leaving them on standby unnecessarily. Run them on economy or don't run them at all if you don't need to. Only run the washing machine when there is a full load. Common sense really.

Food comes into it, as greenhouse gases are sometimes emitted in production and almost always in distribution. There are a lot of environmental issues around food but as far as carbon is concerned a good rule of thumb for everyone is to eat seasonal and local foods if we can. However, it's not simple. Local tomatoes grown in heated glasshouses generate more carbon than those grown in the open and shipped here from Spain. It is worth looking at carefully, or getting someone else to do it for you. For years we bought our vegetables from Riverford Organic Farm, which is local, and delivers fruit, vegetable and meat boxes of seasonal produce to home addresses in Somerset and Devon.

Then there's transport. I walk or use a bike when I can. Or the bus. But that's not always possible. We live in a small town with a bus every couple of hours, none in the evening, and not always going where we want to go. So, do I take the car or not go at all? I make a decision.

On long journeys, we use the car if there are two or more of us travelling together but, if not, we try to go by public transport. But not on planes.

I like flying. I'd love to jet off to Prague or Greece on a plane for the price of a meal out, but it's bad for the atmosphere so I don't do it. We went to Prague once on the train. One day we'll go to Greece. Going to Glasgow or Iona by train or car can be a real slog from Somerset. Sitting in a jam on the M6, I do sometimes think it would be a lot easier to fly. It would be good for me but not good for the next generation.

But that can be turned around. The journey can be about travelling and not just getting to the other end. So, on a walk, I pay attention to what's around me. What I can see. What's growing where. Who the other people are. What's flying around. Become a birdwatcher and there's a lot more to look out for on a journey. Twenty-three buzzards once between Castle Cary and Glasgow.

And on the bus or the train you can read or listen to music as well as look out the window or talk to the person next to you. Be on the journey, not just focused on the destination. It's sometimes easier said than done but that's the idea, and it's a matter of attention.

Paying attention to what is around you and not just being in your head. Being in the present and not the future.

Then there's the house. There are ways of making houses more energy efficient: double glazing, curtains, loft insulation, cavity wall insulation, porch doors. The house I live in now had some of that done before we moved in but we did a bit more, and used some of my retirement lump sum to add PV cells onto the roof. Not everyone has the money to do this, but some things can be done cheaply. Years ago in Durham we put plastic sheeting on the windows, which cut down draughts and bills, and therefore carbon emissions, enormously.

There are possibly grants available for some of these things. And in a rented house you can lobby the landlord to do some of them. If you can think of ways it might save the landlord money – or help them make more – you are, of course, more likely to be successful. But some landlords are responsible about these things and responsive to suggestions.

Houses don't have to be tropical all the time. When I was a child we never had central heating. We dressed accordingly. The winter used to be colder than the summer, indoors as well as out. It still is, in our house. That means we appreciate the seasons. In winter, we light a fire and only have the central heating on when it's really cold.

Theologically, I think there's another important thing that comes into all this, and that is the relationship of law and gospel. It's easy to feel that the need to be green is a new law, weighing down on us. That is a chore for us, and inevitably a chore for other people if we make them feel guilty about their consumption. Or we make ourselves feel good by being greener than everyone else: I'm an okay person because I'm deep green.

I could sit and read in the winter in a woolly hat and a sleeping bag. That would cut my emissions still further. I wouldn't enjoy it but I could feel really good about the fact that I'm doing it. But I don't do that unless there's a power cut and I've run out of fuel. I think Jesus' teaching about fasting calls for attention here. For an example, see Matthew 6:16–18. In fact, the whole conflict between Jesus and the Pharisees and Paul's teaching about the law and the gospel in Romans and Galatians is relevant. Beware the Green Pharisee!

We think about it all. We pray. We make our decisions. And yes, we are still adding carbon to the atmosphere. We can say, 'God, have mercy on us sinners.' We can also say, 'Thank you for all this that you give us.' My natural inclination is to go with the first. I have to deliberately move to the second. And that, I think, is a better place to be. It helps us appreciate what we have, and the more we appreciate it the more we take care of it. And realise, so often, that less is more.

Associate member Lizzie St George e-mailed me:

## Keeping my carbon footprint low, Lizzie St George

Providing food for birds and insects helps to make up for the depletion in natural food because of modern farming methods. My pond and log piles provide safe habitats for newts, toads and slow-worms. My early years were spent on a farm and I'm keen to grow plants that help wildlife in my garden. I produce food that I eat and share with others, and I'm careful to compost or recycle as much as I can. I try to use resources in a responsible way. I have four water butts and a large rainwater container which provide water for the greenhouse, garden and pond. My house is well-insulated and I have 16 solar panels on my roof that generate quite a lot of electricity. Keeping my carbon footprint to the minimum is not always easy, especially as I get older. However, only heating the room I am actually using and only using the car when absolutely necessary should help. I can no longer cycle but public transport offers one an alternative.

## Ethical challenges

Difficult ethical issues remain for the Community as we wrestle with a commitment to reduce our carbon footprint while operating three Island Centres offering radical hospitality to guests and volunteers from across the world. We encourage folk to travel to Iona and Camas when, if taken to its extreme, a commitment to environmental issues would probably dictate a lifestyle in which all travel is local and on foot. We *do* encourage people to use public transport systems, and, as part of our plans to refurbish the Centres, we aim to make the buildings as energy-efficient as old buildings can be. (In 2020, following a successful fundraising campaign, the Abbey Centre was refurbished; this refurbishment includes better insulation and a more efficient, eco-friendly heating system.) But in a world where we have choices, we are still choosing to travel using unsustainable fuels. Yet not to travel at all would mean not being able to fulfil some of our other commitments to justice and peace, and to enable others to have life-changing experiences and to take opportunities back with them to their local communities. For example, Camas, the Community's outdoor Centre on Mull, encourages groups of young people and adults, from all backgrounds, to come and experience living in a place that is largely off-grid. Suddenly, charging phones and game consoles becomes unimportant when people are living with and through the land – growing food, hiking, camping, abseiling, canoeing. All of these things enable people to reconnect and think about the environment in which they live, and to explore how they relate to one another within community.

## Campaigning for change

Other members commit themselves to campaigning at national and international levels. Neil Paynter, editor of *Coracle*, reported on how

Community members, youth, associates and friends joined Scotland's Climate March in Edinburgh in September 2014, walking in solidarity with those most affected by rising global temperatures – and demanding that world leaders agree an ambitious deal at the UN Climate Change Conference in Paris (COP 21) in December 2015.[5]

Diana Hill, an associate member, took part in a pilgrimage to Paris to demonstrate concern and raise awareness at COP 21. She wrote of how *'an unlikely person found herself on an extraordinary mission'*, and described the powerful feeling of joining with groups of pilgrims from around the world to witness the presentation of a petition with 1,800,000 signatures to Christiana Figueres, Executive Secretary of the UN Framework Convention on Climate Change (UNFCCC). Figueres said: *'I was incredibly blessed and privileged, just one day before we began Paris, to receive a very long scroll that was signed by 1.8 million people around the world. Saying: a) we want not just a Paris Agreement, we want an ambitious Paris Agreement and, b) we are doing everything in our personal life to [play] our part in [combating] climate change.'*[6]

Diana wrote to me about her experience:

## 'Pilgrimage2Paris', Diana Hill

All my life I have held a loathing of strenuous exercise. In my schooldays, I would pray for rain so that I'd be spared the humiliation of the tennis court or lacrosse pitch; and in adulthood I would never choose the energetic option. But the concept of going on a pilgrimage was something different. I've taken walking holidays that were quite demanding but each day there was the promise of a comfortable room with good food and a rest day before the next walk. I've enjoyed following the map and noting my progress from point A towards point B. Each year I've stayed on Iona I have walked the island pilgrimage, and most years I have been left with something – a conversation, a sight, the words of a reading or a song – that has proved significant as I have reflected afterwards. The first of these (in 2006) led to a huge change in my life, very painful at the time but ultimately bringing me a move to a new part of the country, a happy marriage and a wonderful job.

More recently I used a 'Columba's Bay moment' to leave behind my fearful self, and that led to my signing up to walk the Pilgrimage2Paris for the Climate Change Summit in November 2015.

Over the years my concern for the future of our beautiful planet has grown, as I have recognised the wounds we inflict on it through our unquestioning habits of consumerism and have heard of the suffering of people all over the world as a result of climate change. My association with the Iona Community has played a big part in this process – as has my role as a volunteer preacher for Christian Aid. A couple of years ago I heard a climate activist from the Philippines speak of the way that climate change is affecting his country, and just last month we heard of five islands that have simply disappeared. So, learning that the Church of England (in which I am a licensed reader/lay minister), CAFOD, Tear Fund and Christian Aid were together organising a pilgrimage from London to Paris to coincide with the start of the 21st session of the Conference of the Parties (COP 21) Climate Change Talks, I felt I had to respond. This was partly as a challenge to myself, but equally to show my commitment to the cause and to try to move the hearts of those participating in the talks to reach an agreement.

Fortunately, my husband, Peter, was of the same mind, so we met our fellow pilgrims for the first time at St Martin-in-the-Fields in London on Friday 13 November, and then we were off. That first day was one of hard pavements, of crowds (some of them specially gathered to encourage us), of traffic lights and road crossings as we made our way from the centre to the suburbs. An early stop we made was at a church in Kennington where primary-school children gathered with their steel band to worship with us. We carried those young smiling faces with us: we were walking for their future.

It was at about that point that the rain began, and it accompanied us for most of the next 15 days. But it was also at that point that we experienced our first act of spontaneous kindness – the local estate agent, across the road from the church, had seen us as the rain began – and rushed out with a box of telescopic umbrellas!

Thanks to meticulous planning we had many stops along the route where we were welcomed in, fed and watered, mainly by church congregations, not seeming to mind at all that we were dripping water and mud all over their floor. Our first stop, for lunch at a church in Balham, showed us just what warm and generous hospitality awaited us. The people from these churches played a huge part in lifting our spirits and encouraging us for what lay ahead. Usually they would pray with us. Often, surprisingly, they would thank us for walking for them. This became a theme that was repeated many times over. I found it both moving and humbling.

After our first night (at Banstead, just inside the M25) we awoke to hear that there had been a series of terrible attacks in Paris. That day and the next we walked holding the people of Paris in prayer, uncertain whether we would be allowed to complete the pilgrimage. We were encouraged to consider how we felt about continuing. But resolve emerged, stronger if anything, and we were then walking not only for climate justice but in solidarity with the people of Paris – not one person chose to turn back. We felt utterly committed, and we had bonded as a group.

We were an ecumenical group, and it had been planned that there would be separate Communion services on that Sunday morning. But thanks to the intervention of the Holy Spirit and some creative liturgy, the Anglican and Roman Catholic priests who walked those first days with us made it possible for us to worship, with integrity, alongside one another; this reinforced our bonding and reminded us of our common purpose. It was a little miracle.

Did I mention the rain? It rained a great deal, and the first three days were amongst the wettest and most challenging, with a great deal of mud! Walking through muddy fields by torchlight, dodging over-hanging branches and potholes, exhausted after two sleepless nights, we wondered whether we would ever reach our host church that Sunday evening. But then we rounded a corner, and there it was, St John the Evangelist in Burgess Hill. And such a welcome, despite our bedraggled state – we were applauded, ushered inside, divested of appalling boots and gaiters and sat down to a delicious meal. The vicar gave each of us prayer beads and the words of the Jesus Prayer – essentials for any pilgrim, he said. And best of all, we could spread ourselves out to sleep anywhere we chose in the warm, newly carpeted church. For many of us that was a real turning point. We slept! And we left next morning restored, encouraged and deeply grateful to the wonderful people who had looked after us there. Another little miracle.

From there, it was up and over the South Downs and into Brighton. Then, battered by Storm Bertie, we struggled along the coast road to Newhaven. That was some battle, with horizontal rain and winds so strong we could scarcely keep on our feet. Next day, with the sea still raging from the storm, we (by now a core group of 30) took the ferry to Dieppe. (I blessed the work colleague whose parting advice to me had been to buy a pack of Stugeron tablets!) In Dieppe we experienced our first taste of French hospitality – a delicious meal from the ecumenical church group, though not before we had earned it by completing a walking tour of the town. Then, thanks to the generosity of an eight-year-old girl who gave up her room for us, a night with a host family, meaning a (very small) bed and a shower!

From Dieppe, our route took us along the Avenue Verte, a former railway line, passing through agricultural land and villages. Hard underfoot, unfortunately, and the rain was still with us much of the time. In France we found the halls were rather more basic than in England; the kitchens were seriously well-equipped but washing facilities left much to be desired. The worst was a concrete complex surrounded by steel fencing, with outside loos and a single cold tap, and segregated sleeping strictly enforced (ironic, given our ages and state of exhaustion)!

But the warmth of the hospitality was wonderful. One shy elderly lady with whom six of us stayed offered to do our washing (very welcome after eight days on the road) and returned next morning with a vast bag, each item beautifully ironed, even the socks! When I thanked her and said we would carry her in our hearts to Paris, she said, 'It was a blessing for me to do it for you.' She welled up as we hugged goodbye, and I confess I did too.

Before we set out I had imagined walking with others, constantly talking – or perhaps telling tales, Chaucer-style. But before long I was thankful that the rain made this impossible: it's not that easy to have conversations when you are all walking with hoods up and heads down. And there was so much to reflect on and give thanks for – the beauty of the countryside, even viewed through rain; the sky at dawn or dusk; the acts of kindness from so many people; and the warmth and friendships that developed with our fellow pilgrims.

Closer to Paris we met people who had been directly affected by the terrorist attacks, some of whom commuted to work in the city. We learned that on arrival we would not be allowed to march or pose for photos outside Notre Dame with other pilgrims, and that some charity groups that had planned to come across to march in Paris had cancelled. Whilst this was disappointing, for me it was the journey that was the most important part and I realised that (apart from the prospect of a good night's sleep) I didn't really want it to end.

I won't pretend it wasn't hard. Especially it was hard on the feet … but no harder on my feet than anyone else's. We encouraged one another and somehow kept going. When I felt tempted to weaken, I felt in my pocket and there was my green Columba's Bay stone, reminding me not to be fearful. Attached to my trusty walking pole was a ribbon saying 'Live, Laugh, Love', which would make me smile through the pain.

Most importantly, what kept me going was the strength provided by people's prayers; we would pray together each morning and most of us prayed silently throughout the day, but I also received text messages from friends telling me that we had been prayed for back home – and that made an enormous difference.

It was liberating to travel light and have all our needs provided for, and to have the time to reflect on how I could simplify my lifestyle. As one who usually dithers in front of the wardrobe each morning, it was marvellous to have the element of choice removed, as we wore the same clothes day after day!

Reaching Paris, we found a city in grief but defiant. Two weeks after the attacks, security was tight. Open-air gatherings were cancelled and security forces were everywhere. But we did meet with fellow pilgrims and heard some astonishing stories: one couple had cycled 16,000 miles from Vietnam's Mekong Delta. Their tales ensured that we retained an appropriate modesty about our own efforts.

We saw Christiana Figueres receive the petition of support – 1.8 million signatures – and the tears flowed as she thanked us for *every single step* which, combined, would stretch seven times round the world. And, as you know, the hearts of the world leaders were moved to reach an agreement, which is why we were walking in the first place.

Our journey was hard (the equivalent of 30 Iona pilgrimages!) and it rained almost every day. But, just as the first Iona pilgrimage I walked (in 2006) brought about a change in my life, this one has changed me too, and despite times of discomfort I wouldn't have missed it. It was a real time of blessing, in so many ways, and that is my dominant memory. Together we were blessed that we all stayed healthy. We were so blessed by those we met on the way, by the prayers and encouragement of those back home, helping to carry us through, and by the relationships we built with fellow pilgrims. I've changed because I put my life on hold for two and a half weeks to do God's work. It wasn't much, but it was what I could offer. And that change in myself is a huge blessing that will be with me for life.

Now the pilgrimage and COP 21 are over, we mustn't get complacent – there is still so much to do! A banner displayed at the Basilica St Denis, close to one of the terrorist attacks, stated: *'La meilleure réponse à la barbarie, c'est de faire face ensemble'* – 'The best response to terrorism is to stand up to it together'. And the best response to climate change is to stand up to it together: every single step we take can make a difference.

### Local community initiatives

Other members work alongside local Transition networks: *'a movement of communities coming together to reimagine and rebuild our world'* (https://transitionnetwork.org). Others are trying to enable local communities to engage with, and do something about, particular environmental issues. Richard Sharples e-mailed me about one such project in Wrexham:

## Community Share Option, Richard Sharples

During the year I invested in a local Anaerobic Digester Project and helped publicise the associated Community Share Option.

A local organic dairy farm has developed a method of dealing with the slurry from the cows. It is 'digested' in a large steel container and the methane produced is drawn off and used to generate electricity. The digestate left over is an excellent plant nutrient and is returned to the land. The benefits are manifold: healthier, organic food; healthier cows; better soil; less runoff; no artificial fertilisers; green electricity; and, most significantly, massively reduced emissions of the gases that lead to global warming, methane being 20 times worse than carbon dioxide.

These plants are now being installed across the UK, based on the design pioneered at Lower Park Farm, Holt, just below Wrexham. A Community Share Option was recently organised in order to raise the capital for a second plant at Lower Park Farm. Such a cooperative model also widens local ownership and awareness. Furthermore, based on known performance, it is likely that those who have invested can expect to receive above-market interest on their capital. So, everybody gains!

This active engagement with community issues and initiatives is a common thread of members' work, as is influencing local churches through teaching and practice. Is this enough though? What is clear is that our world and the natural environment are under threat. Ethical food production is another issue many members are involved with, and this is discussed in the next chapter. Many members have spoken of seeing their role as 'stewards of creation', alongside many others in their communities of course. But Stuart Elliott, an associate from North Wales, e-mailed me to offer a different perspective:

## Participation with creation, Stuart Elliott

Personally, I have tried to stop using the phrase 'stewards of creation' in favour of 'participation with creation' to stress the importance of working with the natural world rather than doing things to it or for it. It also suggests that we might learn something too, rather than us being the ones with all the knowledge and the rest of nature as unintelligent – I've probably spent too much time in the hills!

Stuart went on to share with me 'A song of the earth', a poem he wrote for, and performed at, the Greenbelt Festival 2014, the theme of which was 'Travelling light'. A reminder that the earth beneath our feet is indeed holy ground.

## A song of the earth, Stuart Elliott

You've got dirt on your hands,
did you know?

Euwch, dirty stuff – look at it;

why not look, I mean *really* see
the dark-brown earthy lumps
the dirty brown mess of

complex mixture of old roots and seeds
dead life and potential, the grit and sand

I don't want to touch.

It's gritty, rough, but smoothing and soothing on the skin;
squeeze it in a clump and it crumbles, changing texture and form.

And that smell?

Of burnt ginger cake, rich dark chocolate, old wines
tempting you almost to –
taste is one sense too far!

Oh go on and taste a little of its story.
From where, from what has it been?
Listen to the journey: a thousand plants, animals,
humans, seeds, roots, nutrients grown in changing

exchanging energy within cells and
you were once this earth
here broken down the
dark-brown stuff of life called

'Dirt.'

And we take off our shoes
for we tread on holy ground
and God created the man from the
earth to earth and ashes to ashes
and dust to dust to earth to womb
to be reborn a child of the earth.

That we once were, we shall be again.
The old has been transformed into the new
and back until there is no distinction between us and
the earth which nourishes, feeds and sustains our lives
making us whole and we tread
ever further on her surface each step
pushing down and away, but we cannot escape
so we must embrace the earth
and cherish her warm and welcome womb
enclosing each precious life.
From earth to earth and ashes to ashes and dust to dust
in the sure and certain hope of treading a lighter path
with sister, brother, mother earth.[7]

Stuart Elliott

## Sources and notes

1. From Stuart Elliott's website: www.reluctantordinand.co.uk

2. From 'Our carbon', *Coracle*, the magazine of the Iona Community, 2015, Neil Paynter (Ed.)

3. From a Christian Aid newsletter in 2015

4. From *Love for the Future: A Journey*, David Osborne, Wild Goose Publications, 2013, p.18

5. 'News and letters', *Coracle*, the magazine of the Iona Community, 2016

6. Quoted on the Internet

7. From *Beyond These Walls,* by Stuart Elliott, Lulu, 2015

Growing food for life

*Therefore do not worry, saying, 'What will we eat?' or 'What will we drink?' or 'What will we wear?'*

Matthew 6:25 (NKJV)

Neil Galbraith, a member in Wales, wrote a manifesto of food justice for his New members project. He summarised this for me:

## A manifesto of food justice, Neil Galbraith

Let me, as a grower of foods, as a former chef – one glorying in the smells and colours of allotments and markets – and as a Christian say that the Church has an especial responsibility to find a prophetic voice to speak for the protection of God's creation, its environment, its food. To prophesy – shout from the rooftops – that creation is for all, that good food, good water are for all peoples. That a Christian way of food is food justice for all, not a few.

- Why does healthy food cost more than unhealthy food?

- Why are food bank numbers and users increasing?

- Why are a huge number of people becoming obese because of their bad diets?

- Why do we have periodic food scandals?

- Why does the production of so much of our food entail environmental damage or destruction, including to rainforests in Brazil?

- Why are so many of our 'meat animals' reared and slaughtered cruelly?

- Why have we allowed industrial fishing to endanger huge numbers of fish species?

- Why are we so disconnected from our food, nature, creation?

We have allowed our food culture to be taken over, exploited by corporate capital as a material object of profit so its value to the corporation and to us lies in its external value. And haven't we enjoyed consuming it as well, whether we like to admit it or not? But if it is *'the demonic nature of present systems which force man to consent to his own deepening self-destruction'[1]*, we must free ourselves from the unethically controlling supermarkets and corporations which lead to the environment's and our own destruction; we as Christians and the Church have an obligation to prophesy to its liberation.

We need another way of doing food. If you want to see another version of interconnectedness – ideology and practice – then look to local open-air markets displaying fruits, vegetables and breads down the central streets of large towns, or livestock markets auctioning off cattle, sheep, pigs for slaughter. These are still central to some localities, especially in rural areas or London, which has a food market tradition. But it is not local food markets that dominate, but finance, where corporations trade and expand.

What can we do to change the way in which we 'do' food? We live in a world in which people are often pushed by poverty, time constraints and lack of cooking skills. How does this tie in with our Christian philosophy and commitments?

Stuart Elliott, a member in North Wales, wrote about this in his book *Beyond These Walls*:

## Dirty carrots, Stuart Elliott

Carrots. Which do you buy? I'd like to suggest that it is the 'dirty carrots' that can help bring closer the kingdom of God.

You can buy washed, sanitised, diced, sliced, chopped and bagged carrots if you so choose, and I'm sure they are perfectly good carrots.

But you can also buy 'dirty carrots'. The cleansed ones work just the same, and all you need to do is to open the bag and throw them in the pan. The dirty ones take a little more effort. The soil has to be cleaned off, then they need to be peeled, washed, topped and tailed. In those simple actions, though, we have become closer to the source of our food and actually touched the earth the carrots grew in. We have also become closer to the person who watched over them as they grew and pulled them out of the ground. We give a little back in recognising the grower in these actions. It is the same as choosing fairtrade – choosing to close the loop a little between ourselves and the earth can be no bad thing.

Jesus says *'do not worry about what you eat – so long as you seek the kingdom in all things'*, and as the kingdom is about our relationship with each other and this earth, dirty carrots really can bring the kingdom of God a little closer. [2]

At an evening justice and peace service in Iona Abbey in August 2017, Liz Gibson, a member living on the Isle of Mull, spoke about her life and work:

## The croft, Liz Gibson

I've always liked the idea of growing our own food, but was usually better at the theory than the practice. My mum gardened in the smallest spaces, and moving 20 times in 25 years didn't stop her planting whatever was right for the time of year. So, it's in my genes; but our fingers are still only pale green!

When we were looking to move, we didn't plan to buy a croft. We wanted a good-sized garden and intended to use permaculture principles to grow as much of our own food as we could. Now we have just over 10 acres and it has been every bit the cliché of a steep learning curve. We're encouraged by people who have visited more than once and seen the difference – reassuring us that we have actually 'done a lot'. This year the fruit trees are starting to really crop. We still rely on bought food, but we were self-sufficient in potatoes from July to April, including feeding a lot of visitors. We've hosted more than 300 people in the last four years – some for a night, some for a week or three. Many have been 'WWOOFers' – volunteers through World Wide Opportunities on Organic Farms. Our work may not be called a ministry, but believe me, it is as much one as have been my times as associate minister, hospital chaplain or parish minister. The WWOOFers have been worth their weight in tea. Yes, not gold, but tea. We are amongst the first in Scotland to grow tea for sale. We're very small compared to others, but we're serious.

If we are serious about reducing carbon footprints, and about playing our part in addressing all the food issues we need to, then we have to practise what we preach. Yes, changing the systems at every level is vital, but criticising without changing our own habits whenever possible is hypocritical.

It will be more than whether we do or don't succeed with a personal business. We're not just working on our croft. I'm setting up a social enterprise called Grow Grow Grow, producing food from unused and underused plots of ground.

The Dig for Victory campaign during World War II had people taking food-growing seriously. We can Dig for Peace, or buy from others who are doing so. Maybe not all the time, and maybe not for everything. For now at least, we can still enjoy produce from around the world and contribute our share, preferably things which are best grown in the places concerned. The Iona Community is familiar with the idea of *'a demanding common task'*. We are all different with different callings but we all need to eat. Whatever the main focus of our life we can all be part of making a difference to the food system with every mouthful. A common task that isn't just demanding, but is nutritious and tasty, luxurious even. What's not to like?

## Poppy-seed transfiguration, Stuart Elliott

*Have you seen the seed*
*packets with pictures of prize-*
*winning marrows and flowers*
*in bloom?*

*Like a thousand prisoners*
*those seeds hang on death rows*
*awaiting release sow-by date*
*stamped on each packet.*

*A life sentence without parole.*
*Starving inside foil for freshness,*
*the irony: a seed is fresh when born.*

*I too have held them prisoner,*
*captive since last summer in a*
*jar among the spices and packets*
*of unknown contents on a shelf.*

*Poppy-seeds with a potential to*
*grow into golden patches of sunlight*
*pushing up anywhere they might fall.*
*Is there no justice?*
*For the fruits of the earth bearing seed*
*are nothing if not allowed to grow.*

*Let go the potential that can*
*be held like a seed in the hand.*

*Throw it down, let it go.*

*Let me go, let me grow, let me be transfigured.* [3]

*Stuart Elliott*

## Sources and notes

1. From *Celebration of Awareness: A Call for Institutional Reform*, by Ivan Illich, Open Forum, Calder & Boyars, 1971, p.17

2. From *Beyond These Walls*, Stuart Elliott, Lulu, 2015

3. From *Beyond These Walls*, Stuart Elliott, Lulu, 2015

## Blessing

*Dear God,*
*Creator of light and giver of life,*
*in Jesus, your light has shone out.*
*May your light shine through each one of us*
*that we may be:*

*beacons of justice,*
*channels of peace,*
*agents of reconciliation and*
*bearers of hope.*

John Dale

# Further reading

*Former Leader of the Iona Community Norman Shanks suggests the following books about the Community for helpful material on the origin and development of the Justice, Peace and Wholeness Commitment.*

**Further reading, Norman Shanks**

*The Iona Community: Personal Impressions of the Early Years, Ralph Morton*, St Andrew Press, 1977

Ralph Morton was George MacLeod's Deputy Leader for a few years (and also Warden of Community House, Glasgow) but to some people's surprise was not elected to succeed George as Leader in 1967. I suspect, despite the apparent date of publication of 1977 (in my copy anyway), this book may well have been written and first published earlier. It's interesting that there seems to be nothing at all about the admission of women to the Community in 1969 and very little at all about justice and peace concerns (Community House in Clyde Street, Glasgow housed campaigning and other organisations and had a programme of activities focusing on political and social action); but see Chapter 8, and especially page 127 about '*criticism of and opposition to the Community from its beginning ... on account of its political teaching and actions*'.

*Outside the Safe Place: The Oral History of the Early Years of the Iona Community*, Anne Muir, Wild Goose Publications, 2011

See especially Chapter 8 about 'The Community and Africa'. In both Nigeria and Nyasaland, now Malawi, and later also in South Africa, several Community members, working as Church of Scotland missionaries, were involved in '*political activities*', resulting in some of them being '*banned*' from staying or returning.

*Chasing the Wild Goose: The Story of the Iona Community*, Ron Ferguson, revised edition, Wild Goose Publications, 1998

See especially page 92ff (which mentions the increasing focus and emphasis on justice and peace issues in the 1960s, as the Abbey rebuilding neared completion); pages 104-106 (relating to the formulation and adoption of the Peace Commitment as an addition to the Community's Rule in 1966, after discussions that older members still remember as '*controversial*'); page 124 (referring to the appointment of Helen Steven as Justice and Peace Worker and the opening of Centrepeace in Glasgow); page 164 (an interesting paragraph on the relation between single-issue campaigning and broader political change); and pages 177-178 (on the development of 'area of concern' working groups and campaigning on social/political issues but, interestingly, omitting any mention of the amendment/extension – again involving lively discussion! – of the 1966 commitment to become a 'Justice and Peace Commitment' in 1987/88).

*Iona: God's Energy: The Vision and Spirituality of the Iona Community*, Norman Shanks, second edition, Wild Goose Publications, 2009

See especially Chapter 4, 'The Membership and Rule of the Community' (the Justice and Peace Commitment is specifically referred to on page 81); and Chapter 9, 'Political Engagement and the Pursuit of Justice', which reflects on the fundamental significance of these themes within the life of the Community and gives various examples of how members express their commitment.

*Living by the Rule: The Rule of the Iona Community*, Kathy Galloway, Wild Goose Publications, 2010

Chapter VII ('Action for Justice, Peace and the Integrity of Creation') deals pretty comprehensively with the history, theology and implications of the Justice and Peace Commitment – although with the recent 'modification' of both the Rule and Commitment into their present forms, it is now out of date!

*Pathways for Pilgrims: Discovering the Spirituality of the Iona Community in 28 days*, Chris King (Ed.), Wild Goose Publications, 2012

This little book was prompted by Chris King, who had already produced study booklets on discovering Ignatian, Benedictine, Franciscan and Celtic spirituality in 28 days and wanted to do the same for 'Iona spirituality'. I coordinated/edited this book, with great assistance from several other members, each of us contributing several days. Justice and peace themes permeate the book but are most obvious in 'Week 3: Engaging with the World'.

# About the contributors

*Aabira*, a pseudonym used for writing and campaigning, has worked with Susan Dale for several years now, campaigning for the rights of Muslim women affected by domestic violence. She is also involved in a refuge for Muslim women and children, and in running interfaith groups. Aabira became an associate member of the Iona Community after staying at the MacLeod Centre in 2012.

*Agnes* was a guest at the Abbey Centre on Iona in 2016. She enjoyed participating in the sessions and helping with the common tasks.

*Alyas*, which is a pseudonym, was a guest at the MacLeod Centre on Iona in 2014 and has been in regular correspondence with Susan Dale since then. Together they write and campaign for more understanding of LGBTQ+ issues.

*Warren Bardsley* is a Methodist minister who first went to Palestine/Israel in 2005 with the Amos Trust, and later served as an Ecumenical Accompanier for three months in East Jerusalem. Since then he has returned a number of times. Warren is a founder member of the Kairos Britain movement and co-author of *Time for Action: A British Christian Response to A Moment of Truth, the Kairos Palestine Document*. He is retired and lives in Lichfield.

*Sally Beaumont* is a widow in her 80s, who lives in Glasgow. She has had several passions in her life: her husband Jack (who died in 1998) along with her three children; demonstrating against nuclear weapons of mass destruction with Helen Steven, Ellen Moxley and the 'Horties'; offering rooms in her home to destitute asylum seekers; and especially in her role as a member of the Iona Community.

*Jean Belgrove* is a member of the Iona Community.

*Ruth Burgess* is a member of the Iona Community living in Dunblane. She is a writer and an editor for Wild Goose Publications and a writer for Spill the Beans. She enjoys her garden, which is graced by the presence of a tribe of sparrows and a murder of crows.

*Peter Cope* was ordained in 1966 and served in the Anglican ministry for 41 years, mostly as an industrial chaplain in different urban environments. He became an Iona Community member in 1991, and strongly believes that the churches should do more to serve the needs of the poorest in the UK.

*John Dale*, a retired solicitor and retired Anglican minister, has been a member of the Iona Community since 2012. He was Iona Community's Carbon Coordinator between 2012 and 2014, and was Operations Manager for the Iona Community on Iona for 2019. He is also a husband, father and grandfather.

*Susan Dale*, the narrator of this book, completed a doctorate in education in 2009, specialising in narrative and life story research, and has worked as a psychotherapist, spiritual accompanier, researcher and writer for the last 20 years. She also works part-time for a counselling and psychotherapy professional body as an editor and ethicist. She lives in Devon with her husband, John; they have six grown-up children and seven grandchildren.

*Neil Davies* has retired since writing his contribution in this book but still delivers programmes to groups of offenders, focusing on domestic violence. He feels that the justice system has deteriorated since the privatisation of part of the probation service. He says, *'Sadly, because of cuts in the funding of the service as a result of privatisation, it is those whom we seek to help and support who suffer most of all.'*

*Stuart Elliott* lives with his family at Betws-y-Coed. When not tending to his flock (people, not sheep!), he can often be found running around the hills of Snowdonia and writing poetry reflecting faith and ecology.

*Neil Galbraith* is a member of the Iona Community currently living in the Brecon Beacons in Wales. He produced the manifesto of food justice as part of his New members project.

*Penny Gardner* and her husband, Geoff, met in their late thirties, and became Christians shortly before getting married. Both had careers working with children; Penny as a psychological therapist for CAMHS, and Geoff as a youth leader, who then went on to teach circus skills for 30 years. After their own children, they raised a second family of three, who came to them through fostering. They became associate members of the Iona Community about 10 years ago.

*Liz Gibson* is a member of the Iona Community living on Mull with her husband, Martyn. She is passionate about justice, with a personal focus on the environment. She is a Church of Scotland minister.

*Margaret Hart* is a retired social worker, voluntary sector manager and higher education professional. The Iona Community has been a major influence on her life for 20 years. She found the courage to join the Community in 2012, reflecting the encouragement and support of what she says are *'some inspirational and very human Community members'*.

*John Harvey* has been married to Molly for 57 years. Both retired now, they have a family of four children and six grandchildren and have lived in Glasgow for the last 40 years. John served as a minister in areas of poverty across Central Scotland for much of his working life.

*Molly Harvey* is married to John and is the mother of four and grandmother of six. She was a member of Gorbals Group Ministry (1963-1971), and the Resident Group on Iona (1971-76). She later worked for 15 years as the Project Coordinator of Glasgow Braendam Link, an organisation working in partnership with families living in poverty, enabling them, the experts, to have a voice and to be heard.

*Desirée van der Hijden* lives in Barendrecht, a village just south of Rotterdam, the Netherlands. She has worked as a RC pastor for almost 30 years, first in a parish but most of the time as a chaplain in hospital. Since first visiting the Isle of Iona in 1997, she and her husband have been active within the Dutch Iona Movement

*Diana Hill* is an associate member of the Iona Community and a Reader in the Church of England. She is a volunteer preacher for Christian Aid and lives in Lichfield with her husband, Peter Phillips.

*Mike Holroyd* is a musician and theologian originally from South West England and now living in Scotland. Mike has facilitated many seminars and group discussions on theology, disability and the church throughout the UK and beyond. He currently works for a charity working alongside other blind and partially sighted people in developing community and finding a voice.

*Christine Jones* is a Methodist minister, wife and mother of four, who lives in Chester and volunteers with a food justice network (Cheshire West) where Poverty Truth Commissioners are taking a leading role. Issues of access and inequality have always been central to a journey of faith which has been shaped, challenged and inspired by being a member of the Iona Community.

**Hind Khoury** is a development economist, General Secretary of Kairos Palestine (www.kairospalestine.ps), a former Delegate General of Palestine in France, and a former Palestinian Minister of State for Jerusalem Affairs.

**Susan Lindsay** lives in Fife and works as a gardener. *'I'm standing at the Wailing Wall in Jerusalem, posting a note into a crack in the wall. I squeeze it through the other small pieces of paper ... Now it's August 2017, and I'm standing in the Abbey on Iona being hallowed: a living prayer, posted in the world.'*

**Mike Mineter** bumped into the Iona Community when a windy day delayed a sea kayak trip around Mull in 1989. He spent the next summer leading outdoor activities at the Community's Camas Centre and getting to know the Community. He lives in Edinburgh and works with climate scientists as an expert in high-performance computing.

**Doreen (Dora) Nyamwija** worked at the Iona Centres between 2013 and 2017. Even amidst the challenges that life brings, she still believes that nothing is permanent and that things can only get better. While she was on Iona, Dora raised money to build accessible toilets for children with disabilities in Uganda. See: www.gofundme.com/f/accessloosUganda

**Orthie** is a pseudonym. Since graduating from university, Orthie has worked for an international aid organisation specifically supporting refugees in various countries in Africa, including the Democratic Republic of Congo, where he was born.

**David Osborne** has, among other things, worked in the construction industry in Scotland, taught physics in Nigeria and been a vicar in Shropshire and Somerset, where he was instrumental in developing a diocesan environment policy. Now retired, he is involved with a local green group, fundraises for Christian Aid, chairs a project to develop a medieval church as a community centre, sings in choirs and folk clubs, and writes. He joined the Iona Community in 1996.

*Neil Paynter* is an editor, writer and late-night piano player. Previously he worked in nursing homes and night shelters in Canada, London and Scotland.

*Alison Phipps/Swinfen* is UNESCO Chair for Refugee Integration Through Languages and the Arts and a member of the Iona Community.

*Jan Sutch Pickard*, an Iona Community member, poet and storyteller, was Warden of the Abbey earlier this century. After serving twice as an Ecumenical Accompanier in the West Bank Palestinian Territories, she returned to live in the west of Mull, where she continues to write liturgy and study material for Church Action on Poverty and IBRA as well as the Iona Community. Committed to action for peace and justice in Israel/Palestine, to caring for creation and to confronting the challenges faced by the local community on Mull, she finds that formal statements and frantic e-mails are often less powerful than poetry and prayer.

*John Polhill* is a retired IT Consultant who works voluntarily in the Environmental Team of Lichfield C of E Diocese. In 1999, John and his wife, Christine, bought a home on the edge of Cannock Chase (20 miles north of Birmingham). In the grounds of this property they have created a series of themed gardens on the Christian spiritual journey and environmental issues (www.reflectiongardens.org.uk). The gardens and associated meeting space/retreat accommodation are used regularly by individuals and groups.

*Rosemary Power* has worked in various church ministries, writes popularly on spirituality, history and social justice, and as an academic, on the medieval Scandinavian-Gaelic world and folk tradition. She has lived with physical disability since her twenties.

*Brian Quail:* Prisoner No.133799 Quail, Brian Michael, religion R.C., born 24/03/1938, former Principal Teacher Latin Greek Russian, father of seven, grandfather to fifteen, member Pax Christi, Iona Community, Scottish CND, SCANA, Catholic Worker, Trident Ploughshares, into Russian icons, wildflowers, Bach, curry, reggae, Gaelic, Ravi Shankar, poetry, Gregorian plainchant, beer, history, Orthodoxy, the Georgian language, the Shroud of Turin, Russian Church music, Bob Marley, daffodils, dancing, Dostoyevsky and Mozart.

*Kaz Reeves* is a mother and grandmother, former nurse and health visitor, who was ordained a priest in the Church of England in 2005, with posts in several challenging parishes and two hospital chaplaincies. She describes herself as Black and British, and delights in spaces for silent prayer and the mystical. As an agent for change she works with individuals, groups and communities, as a pathfinder and activist alongside others, of all faiths and none. She has been a member of the Iona Community for 30 years.

*Eurig Scandrett* is an academic, educator and activist in peace and social and environmental justice. He is a lecturer in public sociology at Queen Margaret University, Edinburgh and a University and College Union representative. He convened the Iona Community's working group on Israel/Palestine, and is currently Chair of Scottish Palestine Solidarity Campaign.

*Norman Shanks* was a Scottish Office civil servant from 1964 to 1979, including a two-year term as Private Secretary to the Secretary of State for Scotland. He was chaplain at Edinburgh University (1983-88), lecturer in practical theology at Glasgow University (1988-95), Leader of the Iona Community (1995-2002), and minister of Govan Old (2002-07). He was Convener of the Church of Scotland's Church and Nation Committee (1988-92), a member of the Central Committee of the World Council of Churches (1998-2006) and received an honorary Doctorate of Divinity from Glasgow University in 2005 for services to church and society.

**Ruth Douglas Shanks** trained as a physiotherapist in Edinburgh and worked in St Bartholomew's Hospital, London, and then in the neurosurgical unit of the Western General Hospital, Edinburgh. On returning to work after her children started school (she and Norman have a daughter, two sons and seven grandchildren), she worked first in St Columba's Hospice, Edinburgh and subsequently with children with special needs in Edinburgh and Glasgow. She spent six months as a volunteer at a leprosy rehabilitation centre in Bangalore, India in 1998–99.

**Annie Sharples** grew up in the Iona Community, and studied History and English Literature at the University of Kent. She enjoys reading, baking, cycling and walking.

**Richard Sharples** is a Methodist minister now living in Bristol, where he continues to use a bike as his primary form of transport and is seeking ways of weaving gardening into his ministry. He is married to Biddy Crossfield, a fellow member of the Iona Community, and father of three girls – Annie, Mary and Eve.

**Will Spangler** was born in 1947 in Ohio, USA. In earlier days he studied architecture, was in the US Navy (aerial photo rating), worked in the printing business, lived in an ashram in San Francisco, did land surveying in the high country of Colorado, worked for a civil engineering company, a gas company, and a fitness company. He is now married to Iona Community member Rosie Hague and lives in Scotland. He and Rosie have two girls, who are well on their way in the world. These days William volunteers for several charities and takes care of the house and garden. Rosie is kept extremely busy as a Consultant in Infectious Disease at the local hospital.

*Helen Steven* was a long-time member of the Iona Community, who, with her partner Ellen Moxley, was a recipient of the Gandhi International Peace Award in 2004. Helen died in 2016, aged 73.

*Lizzie St George* believes that visiting Iona made her consider ways in which her Christian faith could be expressed through the way she lived. Her four boys were growing up so she knew she could not visit Iona regularly, so she became an associate member. Local groups have provided her with essential links to the Community.

*Bob Thomas* is a lay minister (reader) in the Anglican Church and a retired teacher of languages. He is a volunteer worker with Friends without Borders, a charity supporting refugees, asylum-seekers and migrants in the Portsmouth area.

*Tryntsje van der Veer* loves language, especially the Frisian, her native tongue. On Iona, she worked on optimising the balance between her private life and work as a psychiatrist, psychotherapist and coach. In her poetry she tries *'to say more with less words, and explore the layers of life'*. She also loves singing, solo and in choirs, and was glad she could practise that on Iona.

*Pat Welburn* is a retired teacher, social worker and guardian and litem. She has three children, four grandchildren and six great-grandchildren. A member of the Iona Community for 38 years, she has a deep concern for peace with justice and is what she calls *'an irritating itch rather than a banner-waving campaigner'*.

*Reverend Professor Stephen G Wright MBE* is a Fellow of the Royal College of Nursing, an interfaith minister, Spiritual Director for the Sacred Space Foundation, and the author of many books and papers on spirituality and wellbeing. After a distinguished career in nursing, academia, the NHS and the World Health Organisation, he now works with organisations developing the practice of healing, spiritual care, conflict resolution and staff support. He is founder of the Kentigern School for Contemplatives in the Cumbria Diocese.